"My Lord" Salisbury

An Eighteenth Century Aristocrat in a Nineteenth Century World

"My Lord" Salisbury

An Eighteenth Century Aristocrat in a Nineteenth Century World

Nicky Webster

Epilogue by Robin Harcourt Williams

Matador
9 Priory Business Park,
Wistow Road, Kibworth Beauchamp,
Leicestershire. LE8 0RX
Tel: 0116 279 2299
Email: books@troubador.co.uk
Web: www.troubador.co.uk/matador
Twitter: @matadorbooks

ISBN 978 1785891 458

British Library Cataloguing in Publication Data.
A catalogue record for this book is available from the British Library.

Printed and bound in the UK by TJ International, Padstow, Cornwall
Typeset in 11pt Garamond by Troubador Publishing Ltd, Leicester, UK

Matador is an imprint of Troubador Publishing Ltd

To my family

Contents

Acknowledgements

I wish, firstly, to thank the 7th Marquess of Salisbury for allowing me to access the unpublished correspondence of the 2nd Marquess which is held in the archive at Hatfield House. This was a great privilege for which I feel most fortunate.

I cannot express too strongly my gratitude to Robin Harcourt Williams, the archivist and librarian at Hatfield during my researches. He has given me unfailing support and encouragement throughout the development of this project. His deep knowledge of the correspondence has been invaluable, as has been his skill in helping me to transcribe words and phrases when the handwriting of the 2nd Marquess seemed quite impenetrable. His reading of drafts and of the final work, and his assistance in selecting illustrations, has been of great help in completing the manuscript. The epilogue, which he has most generously written for the book, illustrates aspects of Lord Salisbury's life which are not covered in the main text, and has put the correspondence into a much wider archival context.

Lastly, but certainly not least, I thank Robert, my husband, who has helped me in numerous ways: finding and acquiring background texts; sorting out my numerous difficulties with computers and printers; ordering stationery; and putting up with the endless piles of books and papers which have cluttered all available space during the protracted writing of this book. I could not have completed it without his unwavering support.

The Cecil and Gascoyne-Cecil Family Tree

Note: G-C = Gascoyne-Cecil

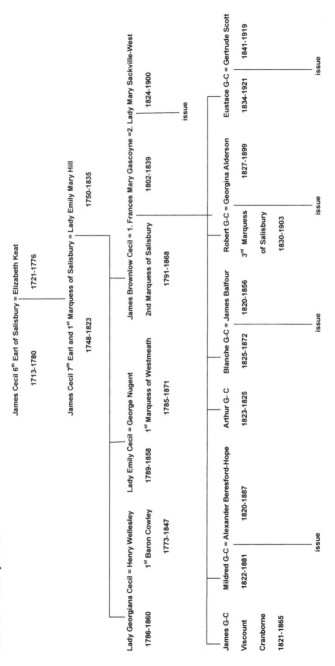

Illustrations and maps

Maps of Hatfield Park before and after the building of the railway: from *Hatfield and its People,* Book 1, 1959, pages 8 and 9.

The 2nd Marquess of Salisbury: print of the portrait painted for the Middlesex magistrates, 1854

The Queen's Visit to Hatfield: print in the *Illustrated London News, 1846*

The Queen's Visit to Hatfield, 1846: Supper in the Marble Hall and Ball in the Long Gallery

BETWEEN PAGES 103 AND 106

Copyright, National Portrait Gallery, London

Arthur Wellesley, 1st Duke of Wellington: after Sir Thomas Lawrence, 1820

Sir Robert Peel, by John Linnell, Published by Thomas Boys, 1838

Edward Stanley, 14th Earl of Derby, by William Walker and Sons, 1864

Copyright, Wellcome Library, London

Edwin Chadwick

With the permission of the 7th Marquess of Salisbury from the collection at Hatfield House

Lord Salisbury in later years

Introduction

Known to all simply as "My Lord", James Brownlow William Cecil, the only son of James Cecil, 1st Marquess of Salisbury, and Lady Emily Mary Hill, was born on 17 April 1791. Styled Viscount Cranborne until he inherited the title as 2nd Marquess of Salisbury in 1823, he died in April 1868, just before his 77th birthday. Having entered public life as Member of Parliament at the age of 22, he had committed his life to the service of his family, his estates, his local community and to Parliament.

Little has been written about the 2nd Marquess, his importance having been overshadowed by that of his third son, Robert, one of the great figures of British politics during the reign of Victoria. He has attracted peripheral interest in biographical texts of the period and is spoken of by historians and by later members of the Cecil family only within the context of the development of the Hatfield estate or as the father of Lord Robert. His character having been reduced to little more than anecdote he has been portrayed as a petty, dyed in the wool, local martinet, yet the massive archive of Lord Salisbury's correspondence held at Hatfield House suggests a different man. Entrenched in his most deeply held views, concerned for the interests of his class, yes. Uncaring of the difficulties faced by those less fortunate than himself, no. Indeed a study of his correspondence with senior politicians, with members of the local gentry of Hertfordshire and with those appealing for his help reveals a deep interest and concern for the common man. The minutes of the sittings of the House of Lords show a thinking member of the Upper House, deeply committed to the Parliamentary process and the rule of law. More intimate correspondence with members of his family portrays a husband, a father, and a brother who experienced the joys, the sorrows and the frustrations of family life and who strove to keep family relationships and fortunes on an even keel.

The period in which Lord Salisbury grew up, raised his family, managed his estates and pursued a long career in Parliament possibly saw more social, economic and political tumult than any earlier period of time. Born during the worst stages of the revolution in France, he and his contemporaries amongst the English upper and middle classes were fearful for their futures. The old Whig oligarchy had given way to a Tory revival which was to last almost without break for nearly fifty years. The revolution in agriculture was changing the old forms of rural society, existence and work, while industrial change superimposed upon the changing landscape was leading to the displacement of families and communities. Pauperism and consequent unrest were increasingly prevalent. The need for reform at local and national level was evident, and Salisbury, from his earliest days managing the estates of Hatfield and in his Parliamentary activities, was a prominent advocate for change which would bring relief to the labouring classes and reduce the threat of popular revolt. But therein lay a conflict. On the one hand he was to become a prime mover behind the great poor law reforms of the early 1830s, on the other he was deeply opposed to changes to the franchise introduced by the Great Reform

Bill. The former was, to his mind, properly the concern of the landed classes whose responsibility for the poor of their communities was a clear duty. The latter was not properly his concern which was, rather, to ensure the survival of the class which he firmly believed was best-placed to make appropriate decisions for government and law. This conflict between the old world dominated by what he perceived to be a benevolent aristocracy and the emerging world, which would be increasingly dominated by a free vote and a free press, would remain with him throughout his life. For a man who played by the old rules of duty, responsibility and self-sacrifice this was an alien and frightening world. The choices for his father before him, and for his sons and their contemporaries who followed, were much clearer. He, standing as he did between these two worlds, endeavoured to live and work according to his conscience and his instincts and it is easy with the benefit of hindsight to judge him harshly.

The man who man emerges from the archive at Hatfield provides a fascinating insight into the personal, social and public life of a senior aristocrat born into the late Georgian era of excess, who lived and worked through the early and middle years of the Victorian period, which saw a fundamental change in the national culture and the founding of modern Britain.

I

A Family Man

"I never heard anything like the manner of living at Hatfield – 500 fed every Tuesday and Friday for six weeks at Christmas, the House full of company eating and drinking all day long". So wrote Sarah Price, mother of the young lady soon to be known as the Gascoyne heiress .[1] It is hardly surprising then, that like many of the aristocratic families who had lived through the profligate years of the eighteenth century, the Cecils were, if not impoverished, not averse to the notion of their son, Viscount Cranborne, making a marriage of financial advantage. The short courtship and marriage of Lord Cranborne to Frances Mary Gascoyne is written of in lively terms by the groom's great-grandson, David Cecil, who describes Frances Mary, the only child and heiress of Bamber Gascoyne and Sarah Price, as representing all the best characteristics of the late eighteenth century English gentry: 'respectable, sharp-witted and cultivated'.[2] She was not a catch to be given away lightly though, and her mother set a family friend, Lord Clarendon, the task of determining the extent of the prospective bridegroom's debts. The sum declared of not more than £4000, of which interest was paid on £3000, was seemingly considered acceptable: even so Mr Leigh, who was drawing up the marriage settlement on behalf of the Gascoynes, did warn that 'men in high ranks of life have of late shown such a turn for licentiousness that too much care cannot be taken to guard against it.'[3] In the case of Lord Cranborne he need not have worried. Whether as a result of the marriage settlement, better financial management, or both, by 1841 the then Marquess of Salisbury could with confidence write to the Duke of Wellington of his desire for a dukedom and declare that 'my fortune is sufficient to support the dignity of the rank I solicit.'[4]

While the Gascoynes would doubtless have held high expectations of the marriage in terms of the social advantages and advancements it would bring, they would have had little reason to anticipate that their daughter was to become the wife, not just of a member of Parliament and a local dignitary, but the wife of a senior member of the Tory elite. Still less would they have entertained the notion that she would be mother of one of the greatest prime ministers of the Victorian period and grandmother to his successor under Edward VII. As for Frances Mary's expectations of the marriage little is known, though one of the few entries in her diary records some fourteen years after the marriage that 'another anniversary has passed of our wedding day: I may indeed regard it as one the most fortunate in my life'.[5] Perhaps, despite the differences in their social station, she found in her husband a reflection of many of her own inherited values. While she had grown up in the educated, solid world of the English gentry, he had inherited the middle-class values of his grandmother, Elizabeth Keet, who had done much to restore the flagging fortunes of the Cecils in the last century.[6] Intelligent, hardworking, shrewd in business and with a 'dominating sense of duty'[7], he was a fervent Tory and deeply committed to the Anglican Church, as was Frances Mary. He was also 'irascible, high-handed and egotistic' and could be 'domineering and quarrelsome'[8]. In the interests of marital harmony and social acceptance her noted personal charm and reluctance to assert herself in public[9] must have provided a valuable counter to the less attractive aspects of her husband's personality.

That the marriage was a success is indisputable. It was also a union beset by deep sadness for both. In the thirteen years following her marriage in February 1821, Frances Mary more than fulfilled the role expected of her, bearing seven children including four boys. But the security of the succession at Hatfield transpired to be tragically fragile. James, the first-born son, who arrived prematurely in late October 1821, was 'afflicted with a kind of nervous debility which, before he grew up, resulted in a complete loss of sight, and which was manifested further in a general feebleness of constitution'[10] and deafness. When James was not yet two years old, his father succeeded to the Marquessate of Salisbury. James became the new Viscount Cranborne and even at this early stage it must have been clear that he was unlikely to live to an old age. Still less was he likely to develop the strength and intelligence which would be required of the heir to one of the greatest estates in England. Not unnaturally, the dynastic hopes of the Cecils came to rest upon the second born son, Lord Arthur. But sadly, if not unusually, he survived for little over a year. Two healthy daughters, Lady Mildred born in October 1822 and Lady Blanche born in 1825, must have been little consolation and Frances Mary lost a further daughter before finally, in 1830, a third son, Lord Robert, brought assurance that the succession was safely secured. His birth was followed in 1834 by that of a fourth son, Lord Eustace.

While large families were the norm in the early to mid nineteenth century, the rigours of childbirth still exacted a heavy price on the health of mothers regardless of class. Frances Mary's diary provides little insight into her relationship with either her husband or her children, focusing instead upon the social scene at Hatfield and in London and at length upon her friend and hero the Duke of Wellington. But Lord David Cecil found the diaries 'in general low spirited and anxious', which he attributed to the deepening concerns about Lord Cranborne[11], while Lady Gwendolen Cecil records that her grandmother's health was always delicate.[12] After the last diary entry in August 1838 Lord Salisbury added the note that 'at this period Lady Salisbury's illness began. She was never really well afterwards and died on the 14th of October, 1839'[13].

The deep affection in which Lady Salisbury was held by all who had known her is easily observable in the correspondence received by her husband during this last illness and on the news of her death. Her daily progress was reported in the press and brought good wishes, offers of help and requests for further news from dignitaries throughout the country, including Princess Mary, the Duchess of Gloucester.[14] Her death brought letters of condolence from, among others, the Earl of Verulam, Lord de Ros, Viscount Ingestre, the Duke of Rutland, Earl Talbot, the Countess of Clanwilliam, Lord Hill, Lord Kenyon, Lady Grosvenor, Lord Granville Somerset, the Marchioness of Exeter, the Marchioness of Londonderry and Ernest Augustus, the King of Hanover. There were also, of course, letters from the local gentry, the militia and the freemasons. Almost all were replied to by Lord Salisbury himself in handwriting which unlike his usual firm hand was shaky and barely legible. Each was a heartfelt expression of his devastation at the loss of his wife of eighteen years. 'The loss I have sustained is to me irreparable' he wrote to the Duke of Rutland. 'As far as earthly comfort can be given in the circumstances of one so wretched as myself I must feel it is in the marked friendship with which you and many others participate in my feelings'.[15]

Marriage of convenience it may have been at the outset, but had there been any doubt about the very real affection in which he had held Frances Mary it was dispelled both by his expressed grief at her loss and in the manner in which he went about the raising of their children after the loss of their mother. He continued their education in the way that she would have wished[16] and he was mindful of their needs when making decisions about his own commitments. While his sons were occupied at school, he felt obliged to keep his daughters with him and was clearly not prepared to leave them in the sole charge of a governess or household servant.[17] Whether because of the closer relationship forged of necessity with his daughters, or because of the more onerous expectations to be nurtured in his sons, Lord Salisbury appears to have borne a clearer affection for Lady Mildred and Lady Blanche than for Lord Cranborne, and Lords Robert and Eustace. Nevertheless, his copious correspondence with friends and family reveals a man at variance with the accepted view of him as remote, domineering and unsympathetic.[18] He was above all a family man, subject to all of the stresses of family life and, later, single parenthood; sometimes impatient, always mindful of duty and responsibility, but whose concern for the welfare of his immediate and his wider family cannot be questioned.

∽

It must have been with some relief to Lord Salisbury when three years after her mother's death his eldest daughter, Lady Mildred, became engaged to Alexander Hope (from 1854 known as Beresford Hope). Similar in age to his daughter, and with a connection on his mother's side to the Marquess of Waterford, Alexander was a respectable match. What is more, already a wealthy man, he had prospects since his widowed mother had married her cousin, Viscount Beresford, which meant that he would in due course inherit his stepfather's estates. Educated at Harrow and Trinity College, Cambridge, he sat in the Commons from 1841-1852 and from 1857-1859 as Member for Maidstone and later for Cambridge University. He was a committed Anglican and Tory like his father-in-law. In replying to a letter of congratulations on the engagement from Alexander's brother, Henry, Salisbury expressed the greatest satisfaction at the connection with the Hope family 'which stands most deservedly high in public estimation and with an individual so much beloved by all his contemporaries'. He was confident he wrote that 'the union will be attended with every happiness'.[19] Well, the marriage was certainly fruitful, Lady Mildred providing her husband with three sons and seven daughters. Whether she felt the same degree of respect for her new in-laws as that expressed by her father was questionable.

Like her father, and in keeping with what was expected of young gentlewomen of the time, Lady Mildred was a great correspondent. Her frequent letters to her father, often written in French and always prefaced with 'Dear Papa', show that she was perfectly confident of her place in her father's affections and, what is more, happy to exploit it quite outrageously. When, a year after her own marriage, her sister Blanche became engaged to marry James Balfour, she complained bitterly to her father that the date set for the wedding was inconvenient as she was in Bath where her husband was taking the waters and couldn't possibly come back to Hatfield. 'I am so selfish as almost to wish that Blanche's marriage was not to take place until about the end of the month'. She wanted all the gossip, though, asking whether all of the settlements were finished yet, 'and how much has Mr Balfour the Father and how much does he give them? I am anxious to know as I have heard such different reports of the amount of his fortune. I hope he will give them a handsome allowance'.[20] In January 1845, her plans for a visit to Hatfield falling foul of her father's commitments found her writing again to 'Dear Papa'. 'What a bore that you have engaged yourself from the 10th to the 18th.' Giving reasons for being unable to come after the 18th she adds somewhat petulantly 'Where are you going to on the 10th?' Two days later she wrote again claiming that he could 'have no idea how much I am vexed about not paying you a visit … there is no chance of your coming to town next week is there?'[21]

Eighteen months later, Hatfield became the focus of much excitement when it became known that Queen Victoria was to make a visit to Hertfordshire. Replying to Lord Salisbury's letter informing her of this, Lady Mildred let it be known that she 'would be very happy indeed to be at

Hatfield for the Queen's visit' for although she didn't 'enjoy Royalty' her greatest happiness was in being at Hatfield. Unfortunately, she felt obliged to ask her father to invite the Beresfords since she thought they would be highly offended if they were omitted and she couldn't see how she could go herself if they were not. There was a way around this, though, she thought, and suggested that her father 'might ask them but tell them at the same time that you are afraid they will be very inconveniently lodged'. A few days later she wrote with a more elaborate plan. 'You can easily say that you would be very glad to see them, but that you hope they will not take it amiss if you treat them without ceremony and that as you have no rooms in your opinion good enough for them, but only rooms high up in the house, and if they did not like those whether they would mind lodging with us in the inn.' She added that she did not think that there was 'the least likelihood of their coming, but the civility is asking them and sending their names in to the Queen'. She was clearly desperate that her plan should be put into action before her husband's parents became aware of a pending invitation, since she pleaded with Papa to send the invitation with its provisos by express, a service which she was even ready to pay for. Salisbury evidently did as he was bid for just one day later he received his daughter's 'thousand thousand thanks dearest Papa' for his kindness. Fortunately Queen Victoria approved of the addition to Lord Salisbury's list of invited guests, but judging by newspaper accounts of the visit the Beresfords did not apparently take up the offer.[22]

Relations between father and daughter were not always so amicable, becoming severely strained over Lord Salisbury's second marriage six months later to Lady Mary Catherine

Sackville-West. It seems that in preparation for the marriage, Salisbury had written to Mildred, letting her know of his intentions and requesting that she should make a suitable announcement of the forthcoming nuptials to the Beresfords. The reason for the ensuing tension, which lasted for a full nine months, was fully described by Mildred's husband, Alexander, when he attempted to sort out the misunderstandings. 'I know you are angry with Mildred' he wrote. 'She did write to announce your marriage to my Mother, and the Marshal, but as was natural she was more interested in the event than in the words, and so failed them'. Clearly the Beresfords had felt that the manner in which the news was conveyed to them was outside 'the conventional rules of society, and of the etiquettes accompanying a marriage', certainly not the kind of formal announcement which they felt should precede any marks of goodwill extended to Lord and Lady Salisbury on the occasion.[23] Salisbury denied feeling the slightest anger against Mildred, and said he had certainly not intended to give offence. His daughter, he said, 'was the natural channel of communication' and he had 'adopted it without any further consideration'.[24] The rift was healed, much to the relief of both, but the episode was a firm reminder of the social niceties of the day and, as now, of the lengthy misunderstandings which can arise from poor communications.

∽

Lady Blanche figures less in Lord Salisbury's correspondence, though the social etiquette surrounding her marriage to James Balfour is touchingly recorded. The ardent suitor wrote most anxiously to his future father-in-law saying that he 'must have seen what are my feelings towards your daughter, Lady Blanche. I love her truly and sincerely and if I should be so fortunate as to obtain yours and her consent to our union her happiness will be the most anxious study of my life.'[25] He left his fate in Salisbury's hands, enclosing for him a note to Lady Blanche which he should deliver only if he had no objection to him as a son-in-law. Salisbury, on this occasion, stuck firmly to the approved etiquette by making it clear in his reply that 'it will be necessary for me to enter into communication with your father and mother before I can give my desired consent.'[26] Consent, of course, was quickly agreed between the two families and Salisbury was within three days of the proposal writing to Queen Victoria informing her of the forthcoming match and venturing to ask her 'to favour me with your good wishes for their prosperity'.[27]

Frances Mary would doubtless have been overjoyed to see both of her daughters settled in suitable marriages, for Blanche had made no less of a connection than had her sister Mildred. Her new family came from established Scottish roots, Balfour's mother being daughter of James Maitland, 8th Earl of Lauderdale; while he, educated at Eton and Trinity College Cambridge, was already MP for Haddington. The union was to last less than thirteen years, since Balfour was to die at the age of 36 from tuberculosis, though not before Lady Blanche had provided the family with five sons and three daughters. It was the first of these sons who was to become the 1st Earl Balfour and Conservative Prime Minister of the United Kingdom after the death of his uncle Robert, third son of Lord Salisbury and Frances Mary.

While his daughters were doubtless of great importance and a source of great pride to him, Lord Salisbury, like every other head of an aristocratic lineage, needed above all to secure the family title and estates through the birth of healthy, intelligent and energetic sons. When, just nine months after his marriage to Frances Mary, his first son was born he must have been overjoyed. But it was to be a short-lived celebration. It has been suggested that James may have been damaged before birth when his mother contracted German measles.[28] Whatever the cause, it was quickly apparent that the little Lord Cranborne was not developing as he should, and was becoming increasingly blind and deaf.

There is very little mention of the young child in the Marchioness's diaries and nothing of note until he was fourteen years old. Unlike his brothers he was unable to follow the usual pattern of education and social development afforded young aristocratic boys. Instead he was placed in the care of a series of tutors and, as he grew older, tutor-companions who accompanied him on an unending sequence of travels around the world. When he was eleven years old and travelling in Italy, Salisbury had written to the boy's physician, Dr. Urquhart, most anxiously asking for news of Cranborne's health. Urquhart's reply was very positive, claiming that the boy was in good health and had 'recovered his hearing perfectly and is in many respects as well as I could wish with the exception of the eyes'. He went on to admit, though, that he didn't believe that he had yet 'any distinct idea of the form of an object by the sense of sight'.[29] Things were not to improve over the next few years. Just before his fourteenth birthday, Lady Salisbury wrote of her regret that 'Cranborne's infirmities increase, and his case appears to me to grow daily more distressing and more hopeless'. In October of 1835, she took Cranborne to town to consult a homeopathic physician, Frederic Quin. Quin was far from reassuring but agreed to see him again the following week. After the second consultation, the desperation of Cranborne's situation and of his mother's feelings really surfaced. 'Cranborne has seen Quin again', she wrote. 'He gives but very slender hopes for his recovery'. And then, 'I am prepared for the worst, and even a fatal termination would be a mercy compared with his present miserable state; but whatever be the result I fear it must be lingering.' She concluded the entry with the information that Cranborne was soon to 'be placed with a clergyman in Devon'. Shortly afterwards Salisbury escorted his son to Devonshire and placed him in the care of Henry Lyte, Vicar of Berryhead, near Brixham.[30]

To send his son away from home and into the care of tutors and carer companions would appear harsh by today's standards, but the Rev. Henry Lyte and his successors James Faithfull and Edmund Johnson, who between them attended to the needs of Lord Cranborne for more than twenty years, would appear to have been chosen with care. Henry Lyte, later known for his poems, sermons and letters; most particularly for his nationally popular hymn "Abide with me"; had experienced separation from his own family as a child, and his natural kindness and sympathy for his young charge is evident in the correspondence between him and the boy's father. Edmund Johnson's care for Cranborne during his twenties and thirties, also shows a genuine understanding of his charge's difficulties and needs. He travelled with him to the principal blind schools of Europe, including Russia; and this before the development of the railways. On his return, with the support of Salisbury, he devoted himself to the welfare of the blind and the deaf and the dumb and he became an important figure in national societies and developments. Though accompanying Cranborne for a much shorter time, James Faithfull undertook a significant journey with him to South America.

When Cranborne first went to into the care of Lyte he was just fourteen years old and he remained with him until he was nearly nineteen. During these years his father kept in regular contact with his son's state of health and tuition through Cranborne's visits to London and Hatfield; in the pre-railway era he travelled by way of steamer from Torbay. Salisbury also conducted a steady correspondence with his tutor. Again, the letters reveal a breadth of concern and involvement in the upbringing of his son which places a different perspective upon his family relationships. Given the changes in the expectations of parents in the 1830s by the time of Lord David Cecil's writing of him in the 1970s, it is hard to recognize the man whom Cecil describes as 'remote and unsympathetic'.[31] Indeed, the correspondence regarding Cranborne's health and academic progress shows genuine concern and careful thought about the best way forward for him.

Lyte's early assessment of his new charge was that he was very quickly 'quite at home with us, and I think the most cheerful person in our house'. He reported that Cranborne had an excellent memory, could retain what he heard and could reason on it. His academic regime consisted of history, geography, English prose and verse, a little Latin, French, Italian, German, arithmetic and Bible studies. He had written an extremely good theme on the superiority of England to all other countries; and Lyte explained to Salisbury in some detail how he intended to create a map with each country's outline indented so that the boy could use his fingers to gain a degree of pictorial representation. Regarding Cranborne's physical progress he reported that he was 'much fatter than he ought to be' and hoped that 'exercise daily' would 'keep his flesh down'. He asked of Salisbury whether he wished any further regime to be adopted to this end.

Salisbury's reply to this long and detailed account of his son's progress was full of common sense. Rather than push the boy to study Greek, which he thought to be out of the question, he felt that the time would more usefully be employed to improve his physical fitness. As for Latin and French, he was convinced that learning through conversation would be 'the best mode of learning', and he asked that in future Cranborne should always address his governess in French. [32]

Six months later every detail of the boy's progress or otherwise was being reported to his father: the arrangements made for his wellbeing while the Lytes were on holiday, the provision for his daily walks, his lessons in mathematics and German and his 'improved appearance'. It was not all good news, though. 'The only thing in which he gets on badly is his writing. He knows all the letters that we received for him, but he can still, though he daily tries, scarcely sign his name'. The report went into great detail about the boy's manners and deportment, Lyte requesting that 'perhaps your Lordship will be so kind as to direct the person who walked with him not to allow his Lordship to lean on his arm – he will want a frequent hint likewise about putting his hands so constantly into his breeches pocket, stooping to eat his bread and butter instead of lifting it to his mouth, speaking indistinctly and some other little matters which your Lordship will soon observe'. The letter ended with a request that a new ear trumpet be sent, so it would seem that his hearing had improved little.[33] When, later, arrangements were being made for Cranborne to go up to town for the summer, he was reported to be in vigorous health, though 'not so much improved in manners or in intellectual matters', since these had, in accordance with his father's wishes, been sacrificed in favour of the boy's physical health.[34] Had Cranborne been a fourteen year old adolescent from an ordinary family, his deportment and manners might have attracted less opprobrium, but for the heir to a great estate this was a persistent difficulty which could not be overlooked.

During the last two and a half years of Lyte's tutorship his correspondence with Lord Salisbury focused more specifically upon those aspects of Cranborne's education which were of the greatest concern. In December 1837, when the boy was sixteen years old, Lyte sent an example of a theme which he had written about the sea. Though the ideas and punctuation were Cranborne's own, he had been unable to write the essay himself and had relied upon a scribe to do this for him.[35] Lord Salisbury was not at all impressed and replied within two days with a stinging rebuke that his wishes for more effort to improve his son's handwriting seemed to have been ignored. 'Other children who labour under a similar affliction learn to write,' he said, and 'I am reduced to think that the neglect of my earnest request must either proceed from some mental incapacity or from a depth of obstinacy which I can only look to you to overcome'.[36] A few weeks later a further sample of work was sent with the earnest hope that 'your Lordship may be able to discern in it some promise for the future'.[37] This time the reply was more favourable since Lyte reported that Lord Cranborne 'was greatly delighted and encouraged by your Lordship's last message'.[38] This more direct intervention by Salisbury continued until the end of the tutorship in the summer of 1840, almost a year after the death of Frances Mary. Just how Lyte felt about the constant stream of instructions can only be imagined. His replies to Salisbury make it quite clear that he was expected to pursue all of the suggestions arriving from Hatfield most assiduously. In October 1838, thanking Salisbury for 'his kind and valuable' letter, he declared his intention to act on every suggestion and asked that he be 'favored occasionally with more of the same kind. It will, I am sure, be a great encouragement and stimulus to him to be allowed to write to your Lordship as you propose. I only fear that you are imposing too heavy a task on yourself, with the manifold engagements which you now have'.[39] A few months later he wrote again, explaining that, though his charge was continuing to improve, he had a tendency to go into too much detail in his dictation and to stick too firmly to the source of his information when writing on a theme. He could fix the minutiae in his mind but was unable to generalise or to understand comprehensive views. His writing was 'still rather careless'.[40]

Nearly a year after his mother's death and having reached the age of eighteen, Cranborne was set to return to Hatfield and Lyte wrote a final letter to Lord Salisbury letting him know that his eldest son was looking forward to seeing him and 'entering on the new field that is before him'. He also made reference to using the remaining time with his charge 'in preparing him, as far as I can, for his new position'.[41] In fact, of course, the kind of 'new position' could not be that usually expected of the eldest son of a great family: a commission in the army, a career in politics, a growing responsibility for the management of the family estates. Indeed, within six months, Cranborne had resumed his love of travel and Salisbury was receiving letters on his health from his then companion James Faithfull. By the time he was twenty six years, little had changed and Salisbury had finally to face the hard truth that while his son would, if he outlived him, inherit both the title and the estates of Hatfield, he would never be competent to take on the huge responsibilities of a great landowner. Had Cranborne been certifiably incompetent it might have been possible within the laws of inheritance to have settled the title and estates upon his second living son, Robert, but this was not the case.

The letter which Salisbury wrote to Lord Cranborne, dated 16 December 1846, when his twenty six year old son was travelling in Italy, is unfortunately missing from the archive. It is possible, though, to piece together from the correspondence between Cranborne and his father the proposal which Salisbury had put to him as a possible solution to the difficulty and of the far from favourable response which it evoked. It would seem from the reply which Cranborne sent from Rome on 25 January that his father had asked for his opinion regarding a possible resettlement of some or all of the estates upon his brothers Robert and Eustace and for his brothers to be given power to act for him. Not only was Cranborne quite adamant that he would not consider such a proposal, but the tone of the dictated reply was full of anger, towards Robert in particular. 'If my brother Robert possesses talent', he said, 'I should think he could make his way well enough without the assistance you propose and I recommend him most particularly, as a second son, to enter the Church, as we have many good livings to offer him'. It was also clear that Salisbury had raised with him the question of his incessant travelling, to which Cranborne replied that while he had no objection to settling in England he would only be prepared to do so if he could live independently as he did abroad. While the response to the first two issues might have been expected, his father was clearly not prepared for a further point raised by his son. He was not prepared to make sacrifices for Robert, he said, since 'I have a strong idea of marrying at some future period. I think it would be extremely hard for my son, if ever I had one, that he should be deprived of the Estate by any concessions which I might in my youth have made'.[42] A second letter received by Salisbury at the same time came from Cranborne's next companion, Edmund Johnson, to whom he had dictated the letter to his father. Had Salisbury been under any illusion about his son's feelings on the matter, Johnson left him in no doubt at all. The impression made upon Lord Cranborne by his father's recommendations had been 'anything but what I would have wished, as he became very low spirited, nervous and poorly...I feel sure that all that could be said in favour of your plans would never induce him to make the sacrifices required as I believe that he would never give the least power to his brothers to act for him, nor would he bear the least restraint.' His charge had 'lost all his former favourable opinions of Lord Robert', he wrote, and regarding Cranborne's possible return to England, he was sure 'that after a month or two he would feel tired and disinclined to remain'. He confirmed, though, that he had 'a great idea of having his own house' despite the financial impossibility of such a scheme and had declared his intention to marry if the opportunity arose.[43]

Salisbury's following letter to Cranborne was conciliatory in regard to the proposal for the estates, 'I think you are quite right in exercising your own judgment upon the proposal I make to you and I carefully avoided in my letter expressing any wish upon the subject'. On the issue of his desire that Cranborne should live in England, he was not prepared to give way. 'My desire that you should live in England was grounded upon the wish that I entertained that you should become as far as your circumstances would permit acquainted with the duties which will devolve upon you after my death. A separate establishment which you seem to desire would entirely defeat this object and I cannot be expected to make a sacrifice to give you this'. Clearly stung by Cranborne's open antagonism towards his brother, he went on to remind him that 'your allowance is at present larger than is usually given to those elder sons who have a home offered to them and under present circumstances cannot be increased more especially as I must look to a provision for your brothers for whom you do not appear to entertain much affection'[44]. He did not in this letter make mention of his son's desire to marry. To Johnson, though, he wrote of his regret that it should have entered Cranborne's head that he should marry, and made it quite clear that he would do all in his power to prevent it happening. 'With his imperfections it is not very likely that he should find any person who would marry him for himself or with whom I should approve of an alliance and unless I did approve of it it need hardly be said that I should neither increase his allowance nor enable him to make any settlement.'[45] By the time Salisbury received Johnson's reply to this in early March, Cranborne was already making plans to leave Rome for Naples. 'I fear', Johnson wrote, 'that nothing will ever induce him to become a settled man, even for the best comforts of Hatfield or London'. On the possibility of marriage he put Lord Salisbury's fears to rest with the assurance that 'I think it an impossibility under the present circumstances, for I studiously avoid his making any female acquaintances'.[46] Whether because of Johnson's assiduous attention to duty or Salisbury's determination to make the prospect of marriage unprofitable, Lord Cranborne never married and he died without issue in June 1865 at the age of 42.

It would have been difficult for Salisbury not to have felt some degree of relief at the death of his eldest son, since the succession to the title and estates of Hatfield was now secured in the person of his second surviving son Lord Robert Arthur Talbot Gascoyne-Cecil, the new Viscount Cranborne, and his three healthy grandsons through Robert's marriage to Georgina Alderson. This was not to say that the relationship between the new heir and his father had been continuously harmonious, far from it. Throughout the boy's childhood, adolescence and early career, there had been difficulties which have been laid largely at the door of the father. Lord Salisbury's great grandson, David Cecil wrote of a young boy who found 'it hard to adapt himself to life; on the one hand hypersensitive and precociously intellectual, on the other clumsy, sickly and unsociable', and claimed that his parents did little to help him.[47] His mother died when he was nine years old, and his biographer, Andrew Roberts, wrote that 'at precisely the time when he most craved affection, the young boy found himself starved of it'.[48] Both Cecil and Roberts describe the horrors of his educational experience, firstly from the age of six at the Hatfield boarding school of Mr. Faithfull and then, from the age of ten, at Eton. Lord Robert's daughter, Lady Gwendolen Cecil, also writes of her father's hardship at this time, describing him as 'a nervous sensitive child in mind and body, with a passionate temper and a craving for affection which was no doubt as unspoken as it was at that time unconscious'. His mother's death was an 'irreplaceable loss to a child of this temperament' and 'not mitigated by the strenuous system of education which then prevailed'.[49] That the system was brutal and damaging to a boy of Robert's nature is indisputable, but it was not the case that his father was uncaring about his son's unhappiness. When Salisbury discovered that Mr. Faithfull, in whose school the young boy been placed, had taken Robert to task for playing games on the Sabbath he intervened forcefully. 'It is my misfortune to differ with you upon the degree of strictness with which the Sabbath is to be observed…knowing what my opinions are you should have warned me before I sent my boy to you that you would feel it your duty to inculcate ideas of right and wrong at variance with my actions.'[50] David Cecil, Andrew Roberts and Lady Gwendolen all quote from Robert's letters to his father complaining about the bullying to which he was later subjected at Eton, but while Cecil and Roberts claim that Salisbury did little to intervene and, by implication, did not care about the fate of his son, Lady Gwendolen having quoted a letter which Robert concludes with 'the pitiful apology, "I know that this is very little interesting to you, but it relieves me telling it to someone", judges the matter more kindly within the context of the time. 'The implied reproach was not deserved' she wrote in 1921, 'Lord Salisbury was evidently shocked and did what he could within the limits imposed by a paternal sense of the value of discipline'.[51] Eventually he removed Robert from Eton and arranged for him to be tutored at home at Hatfield until he went up to Christ Church in 1847. But, since a year had passed since the bullying of which Lord Robert had complained, his departure may have been unconnected.

It is scarcely surprising that during the period of Frances Mary's last illness and her death, Salisbury was unable to give the fullest attention to Robert. Not only was he quite devastated by the loss of his wife, but he had the care of his other children to consider. It is difficult to imagine just how overwhelmed he must have felt when left caring for an eldest son and heir who was clearly never going to be physically fit, a younger son of just five years old, and two teenage daughters. A middle son who was needy and complaining must have been difficult to bear, and things were only to get worse as Robert moved from adolescence to adulthood.

It was when Robert came down from Oxford, that his career ambitions and his attitude towards the responsibilities which accompanied the comforts and advantages of Hatfield became the dominant focus of the relationship between father and son and it was the conflict of views on these matters which led to the estrangement which lasted until 1864, just four years before Lord Salisbury's death.

As Viscount Cranborne, Salisbury had wished for nothing other than to become a professional soldier, but as the only son of a great family this was not permitted and, instead, his mother set about canvassing the seat of Hertfordshire for him. Having failed to win sufficient support for either the County or the Borough of Hertford, he was successful in Weymouth, which he represented in the Commons from 1813 until the election of 1817, when he did succeed in winning Hertford which he retained until his accession to the Marquessate and a seat in the Lords in 1823.[52] He, thereafter, devoted his energies to the management of his estates, and to all of the responsibilities expected of a peer: the Herts Quarter Sessions, the Herts Militia, Lord Lieutenancy of Middlesex, Chairman of the Board of Guardians of Hatfield and, of course, an active presence in the Lords. Lord Robert, though, made it abundantly clear from the time of leaving Oxford at the age of twenty that such a life was not for him. After a brief trial at the Bar, he left Lincoln's Inn to embark upon a two year journey around the British colonial possessions covering Cape Colony, Australia, Tasmania and New Zealand. On his return he rejected a career in law or holy orders and settled for an unopposed election to the pocket borough of Stamford. All of his election expenses were paid by his father who also settled on him £300 per annum, this being interest from money held in trust for him from his mother's estate, plus a further £100 per annum from Salisbury's own resources.[53] The ongoing election expenses were a continual demand upon the Hatfield estate and Salisbury's irritation and disappointment with his son's attitude was to lead to an open rift between them.

Unfortunately, the issue of expenses was not the only source of disagreement. Lady Gwendolen observed that 'never indeed were two men of the same blood more hopelessly antagonistic in all their tastes and interests'.[54] Certainly, so far as Parliament was concerned, Robert and his father held vastly different views. While Robert had 'a profound disbelief in the capacity of legislation to affect the state of the human soul, which was in itself the only thing that truly mattered in life'[55], Salisbury was heart and soul a parliamentarian and saw it as his duty to play his part in ensuring that the legislative programme would support not just the interests of his class, but his country's social and economic wellbeing. While Lord Salisbury most conscientiously attended to the responsibilities of his offices, Lord Robert showed nothing but contempt for his constituents declaring to his brother Eustace that 'a hotel infested by influential constituents is worse than one infested by bugs. It's a pity you can't carry around powder insecticide to get rid of vermin of that kind'.[56] In 1855 he was writing to his father complaining that his Commons work exposed him to nerve attacks made even worse by the suggestion that he might accept the offer of a commission in the Herts Militia.[57]

While differences of attitude towards their responsibilities was a major cause of the rift between the two it was the question of marriage which sowed the deepest seeds of disaffection; the first being that of Lord Salisbury to his second wife, Lady Mary Catherine Sackville-West, daughter of the 5th Earl De La Warr, in 1847, the second of Lord Robert to Georgina Alderson, daughter of Sir Edward Alderson, in 1857. That Lord Salisbury should wish to remarry was not unexpected, neither was the young age of his twenty three year old bride, according to the norms of the English peerage of the time. Tensions between Robert and his step-mother were to be expected, but they were exacerbated by claims that money left by his mother was being settled upon his father's new family. It was also claimed that the second Lady Salisbury showed a clear preference for her own children of the marriage.[58] While the latter accusation might be excused as a human reflection of maternal interest, the accusation of financial misuse was much more serious and came to a head over Lord Robert's determination to marry outside his class and to no financial advantage. When he flung the accusation at his father that he was 'quite sensible that if you were in my place this marriage would be a very unwise one' Salisbury took this to mean that his own first marriage to Frances Mary had been a purely financial arrangement. Robert quickly retracted the statement, but the damage had been done and Salisbury responded by promising to withhold the £10,000 held in trust for each of Frances Mary's younger sons. Robert responded in turn by insisting that the marriage would go ahead despite his father's threats and it duly took place in July 1857.[59]

According to Andrew Roberts, 'the rupture took seven years to heal'[60], but this view is refuted by Salisbury's granddaughter, Lady Gwendolen, who wrote that 'the estrangement between father and son – which never reached the point of a quarrel – was very temporary. In letters not intended for the young man to see, the father's affection for him and distress at the difference which he himself had so needlessly provoked are very apparent'.[61] As for the money, she claimed that the newly married couple 'had sufficient not only for their wants but for most of the luxuries which they valued'. Indeed, Robert was still in receipt of the interest on his mother's fortune and the further £100 from his father.[62] Moreover, his wife's personal fortune brought a further £100 and his prolific writing of articles and reviews earned him a significant extra amount. Altogether, according to Lady Gwendolen, the couple were in receipt of £700 a year which was a considerable income at the time. Finance did become tighter after the birth of a son to Lady Robert in October 1861, at which point Salisbury not only resumed payment of all his son's election expenses but 'helped generously at the time of his wife's confinement'.[63] As for the issue of Frances Mary's bequest, in accordance with her will Salisbury was entitled to the use of the portions left to the younger sons until his death and, as the terms of his own will revealed, he had ensured that wise investment left the portions intact and his sons' inheritances secure.[64] This, as it turned out, was just as well. Robert had complained at the time of his marriage that, if he could invest the £10,000 himself, he was sure that he would obtain a better return than the 3% it was attracting at the time, a claim which seems misguided in view of the abysmal showing of his later investments. His fortunes improved considerably when, in June 1865, he succeeded his elder brother as Viscount Cranborne and when the following year he became Secretary of State for India in Lord Derby's Government, a post attracting a considerable ministerial salary. Free of financial restrictions, he invested heavily in some ill-chosen ventures, though, and the financial woes caused by the spectacular bankruptcy of the prestigious bill-brokers and discount bankers Overend and Gurney were compounded by his resignation from his ministerial post. This deprived him of a major part of his income and between May 1866 and July 1867 he was again begging his father for assistance, this time to a total of £2,750. It was in order to repay the debt that, a few months before his father's death, he accepted the offer to become Executive Chairman of the Great Eastern

Railway, a position which he managed successfully for four years.[65] It must also be said that after his accession to the title as 3rd Marquess of Salisbury, his commitment to the duties of the estate improved significantly.

∽

Lord Salisbury's youngest son by Frances Mary, Lord Eustace Brownlow Henry Gascoyne-Cecil, was probably the most like his father or, rather, as his father would have wished to have been. For unlike his father there were no obstacles to his pursuing a career in the army. From his early twenties he served with the Coldstream Guards, saw service in the Crimea and within six years rose to the rank of Lieutenant Colonel. Having retired from the service in 1863, he sat as Member of Parliament for Essex constituencies for twenty years. Moreover, unlike his brother, Robert, he made a favourable marriage to Lady Gertrude Scott, a daughter of the Earl of Eldon. Also, unlike his brother, his childhood temperament was apparently neither oversensitive nor excessively needy. Eustace's Harrow School report, when he was aged twelve, was not encouraging. Having failed his examinations for Remove he was to be held back for a further term. His master noted that he did 'require considerable stimulus to overcome a certain apathy and listlessness of disposition which seems to prevent his exerting his powers to the utmost'.[66] Salisbury replied, apologizing for his son's indolence and expressing the hope that 'you will take the earliest opportunity which any neglect of his may afford to tell him that he will lose the fifth form again and not to let his disappointment this time operate upon the decision at the next examination. Let it be formed upon his merits'. A further comment on his son's temperament is revealing. 'I observe that you mention his being a little riotous. Except for the trouble which it may give you I do not care for this. A good thrashing from his school fellows or a flogging from his master will soon set that matter to rights. His temper however requires watching. Much may be done with him by gentleness but he must not be allowed to think that he can get the better of you on the slightest occasion.'[67] Two years later, Eustace made his departure from Harrow, though not under circumstances similar to his brother's departure from Eton. Having decided upon a career in the army he was to proceed to Sandhurst and his father must have been pleased to receive a final report and leaving certificate which stated that 'I have never seen anything in Lord Eustace's conduct which could give me a moment's uneasiness, and little to find fault with, save some want of energy in his work'.[68] Seemingly, either the Harrow regime coupled with Salisbury's advice about his temper and the beneficial effects of flogging had paid off, or his temperament was seen as no obstacle to Sandhurst and an army career. His father's approval of his younger son was reflected in his last will, which, over and above the settlement of Frances Mary's estate, made provision in 1857 for Eustace to receive the sum of £220,000 on his death, while a further codicil was to settle upon him all of the River Lee Bonds or Securities for money under the seal of the River Lee Navigation Corporation dated prior to 1865, a very substantial inheritance indeed for a younger son.[69]

The 2ⁿᵈ Marquess of Salisbury: portrait when Lord Cranborne, by
R.T. Bone

(0588)

The 2nd Marquess of Salisbury: by J. Lucas, 1844

(191)

Frances Mary, Marchioness of Salisbury: by Sir T. Lawrence, 1829

Lady Mildred Beresford-Hope (00579)

James, Viscount Cranborne: photograph with Edmund Johnson (0580)

Lord Robert Cecil aged 27: photograph c. 1855 (P1110553)

Lady Westmeath (Emily 001)

Mary Catherine Marchioness of Salisbury: (afterwards Countess of
Derby), portrait by J.R. Swinton, 1850

(00587)

As a senior member of the aristocracy and the patriarch of an important dynasty, Lord Salisbury considered it his responsibility to ensure the welfare not only of his own sons and daughters but that of his sisters and cousins and their respective families. Even here, with the exception of his elder sister, nothing was easy. In 1816 Georgiana had become the second wife of Henry Wellesley, younger brother to Arthur Wellesley, the Duke of Wellington, through whose influence he was in 1828 created Baron Cowley of Wellesley. Throughout the marriage her husband pursued a distinguished diplomatic career, serving as Ambassador to Spain, Austria and finally Paris, where he died in 1847 just a year after his retirement. The relationship between brother and sister appears to have been perfectly amicable and, of course, did much to ensure a strong relationship between Salisbury and his friend and mentor Wellington. Georgiana's younger sister, Emily, three years the senior of the then Viscount Cranborne, was a different matter.

When Cranborne was twenty one years old, his sister Emily made what his family considered to be a highly unsuitable match when she married George Nugent, Lord Delvin, heir to the Irish 7th Earl of Westmeath. Not only was he considered impoverished when compared with the wealth of the Cecil family, he had fathered a child by a mistress in Ireland. Nevertheless, for the first two years of the marriage in 1812, the pair appeared outwardly to be contented and very much in love. Moreover, during that time the couple's fortunes had increased considerably. In 1813, Emily's aunt, Lady Anne Cecil, died and left her niece considerable assets in plate and jewellery and £12,000 to be paid to her on the death of her father. The following year George's father died, leaving his son in possession of the family estates. These inheritances, added to Emily's already generous marriage portion, should have permitted a comfortable living for both. But by this time the marriage was already in difficulties. Mismanagement of the estates led to financial arguments and following the birth of their first child, Rosa, Emily discovered that George had fathered a second child by his mistress in Ireland and was supporting this second family while she was living in far from luxurious circumstances at the family seat of Clonyn. The conflict over this was temporarily patched up with George promising to end the relationship with his mistress and her children. He and Emily then embarked upon a nine month trip to France, during which she proceeded to run up huge debts. In 1817 she was forced to throw herself upon the mercy of the Cecil trustees who advanced her £3,600 from her aunt's legacy as a loan to pay off her debts and to finance an establishment in London. It was a short-lived respite from her marital difficulties, though, for a few months later she left George, taking Rosa with her, and declared her intention to sue him for a legal separation on the grounds of cruelty.

There followed a further reconciliation, largely due to the pressure of her parents who wished above all to avoid a scandal. In return for lifting her threat to sue George and for agreeing to resume normal marital relations, she secured a written indenture by which George was to settle on Rosa the £5,000 marriage portion contributed by her mother and also the inheritance of the Nugent estates if he and Emily did not produce a male heir. By a second indenture George also agreed that, should Emily separate from him at any future time, he would concede custody of his daughter and he would pay Emily an allowance to pay for Rosa's education and maintenance. The first agreement was considered unusual by the Cecil family lawyer, William Sheldon, the second shocking. Whatever the legal niceties, which were later to be fought over bitterly and at length, the peace they bought lasted less than six months. By March 1818 Emily was pregnant again; in May she left her marriage for good and George was immediately presented with a second separation indemnity. This, which he finally signed in August, gave Emily a generous separation allowance and custody of both Rosa and the son born in November.

It was at this point that the relationship between Emily and her family began to break down. Again pressured by the Marchioness and Sheldon, Emily was persuaded to allow George to reside in an apartment in her house and so make the separation less public. She was assured by Sheldon that this would in no way jeopardise the indentures George had signed, but this was to prove poor advice which was to tell against her in her later struggles in court. Also to tell against her was the testimony of her mother who openly criticised her daughter, a betrayal for which Emily never forgave her. When in 1823 her father died, Emily attended the funeral at Hatfield but all attempts to bring about a reconciliation between her and her mother failed. Three years later she ended all contact with her elder sister as well.

Where the then Lord Cranborne stood in all of this is less clear. Certainly he, like his mother, was anxious to spare the family a scandal. Against his will he had been made a trustee of Emily's fortune and she clearly felt that as such she had a right to his support and roundly denounced him when he failed to give it. When the struggle for custody of Rosa commenced, though, he was given little choice but to intervene, both for and against the interests of his sister. In early 1819 George had appealed to the family friend and relative, the Duke of Wellington, asking him to persuade Emily to return to him and to annul the two deeds of separation of 1817 and 1818. The upshot was far from anything the Duke could have envisaged since George chose to interpret his visits to Emily for the purposes of conciliation as evidence of adultery and threatened to bring a lawsuit against him. Whether this was a genuine misconception or a threat designed to force Emily to accede to his wishes, Cranborne felt unable to stand by and see his friend and mentor dragged through the courts. Equally concerned for Emily's and the family's reputation he pressed her to give in to George's demands, and further counselled her against a custody fight in which George's accusations against the Duke could be used against her. Certainly, Emily had cause to feel that her happiness and that of daughter were being cast aside in favour of the family fear of scandal, but her judgement of her brother failed to appreciate the situation in which he found himself and also the extent of the support which he had given her previously.

In the spring of 1819, in a desperate attempt to get Emily to return to him, George had taken both children away to Clonyn and ceased payment of the agreed separation allowance. A few months later Emily learned that her baby son was seriously ill. Despite his opposition to the separation, Cranborne accompanied his sister to Ireland and, finding the child already dead, he effectively pressurised George into surrendering Rosa to Emily and extracted his promise not to demand her back again. Both the promises and the indenture proved false, though, and a year after the children had been taken to Clonyn, Rosa was again taken by her father. Emily immediately fought for the return of her daughter in the Court of Common Pleas, but the case was found in favour of George and the child was removed permanently from her mother's care.

The Case of Westmeath v. Westmeath was pursued through the Secular and Ecclesiastical Courts for fifteen years and involved charges and counter-charges of adultery and perjury, which must have delighted London society and appalled family and friends. In 1827, Emily was finally granted a separation on the grounds of George's cruelty and awarded alimony for life of £700 a year. This, of course, was much less than the £1,300 she claimed through the separation deeds of 1817 and 1818, which were declared invalid by the House of Lords in 1831, and was reduced still further to £315 a year in 1834, following George's successful appeal to the Judicial Committee of the Privy Council. The legal costs for both sides were enormous.[70]

So Emily won her freedom from her husband, but at a huge financial cost and the total loss of her daughter. To her death she never forgave her family for their failure to support her in her battle for separation and financial independence. She had good reason to so revile her mother and the Cecil lawyer, Sheldon, whose poor advice was a significant factor in the failure of the separation indentures. But, when she drew up her will in 1855, some three years before her death, it was her brother who attracted the greatest ire. She still refused to acknowledge that as trustee he had been unable to support her unreservedly or obtain the alimony to which she felt entitled. In the intervening years Salisbury (2nd Marquess from 1823) had made heartfelt efforts to repair the relationship but to no avail. Following the death of Frances Mary in 1839 he wrote of how the death of his wife had left him broken hearted and hoping 'that this renewal of correspondence might afford Georgiana and myself an opportunity to put an end to the estrangement which has so long existed between you and us'.[71] The reply was not encouraging. Having expressed her sorrow at his bereavement and assuring him that she most truly felt for him, she made it clear that her view of his role in her reduced situation had not moved one little bit. 'The possibility of a change in our present relations' she claimed 'lies entirely with you – for I unfortunately cannot adopt a different course so long as I retain the slightest regard to, not only what is due to myself and my own character , but ... truth and justice.'[72] It seems that Salisbury sent the letter to Mr. Faithfull, whose view of the situation was that 'it does indeed appear to close the door of reconciliation' since she 'requires you and Lady Cowley to take her part against one whom she charges with offence against her – and to make her cause – in all respects your own'. He added that while this was impossible could not 'the subject be dropped entirely between you?'[73] Certainly Salisbury listened to the advice and did try again, but not for another three years, when his daughter Mildred's engagement presented a suitable opportunity. 'My dear Emily' he wrote. 'Though unfortunate circumstances have divided us for many years I trust you will receive with pleasure the announcement of Mildred's marriage to Mr Alexander Hope ... I need hardly add that I embrace with pleasure every opportunity of reconciliation with you.'[74] But Emily was not about to give in and after a terse message of good wishes for her niece's forthcoming marriage launched into a tirade of bitterness against her brother. 'Pray take time to read the printed documents which accompany this. I also enclose copies of the whole of the correspondence which has taken place with Lady Rosa.' After going into great detail about her trials and tribulation regarding her daughter, her marriage and her separation and listing everything in which she felt her brother had failed her, she returned again to the trusteeship. That this had been thrust upon him unwillingly when he was only twenty one years old was not a consideration. 'After all the question between you and me lies in a nutshell – a trustee's line is a very simple one. He does his duty to the person he is trustee for'.[75] Salisbury's reply shows more than a little irritation at his sister's complete intransigence. 'I have nothing with which to reproach myself and I ask for no concession from you' he wrote. 'I am determined, therefore, not to enter into any discussion upon the subject .' …'The responsibility of perpetuating a quarrel which ought never to have existed between us must rest with you and I can only hope that further consideration will induce you to enter into our views'.[76] In a final salvo, she threw his own words back at him and ended the correspondence with her deep regret that he had declined the opportunity she had given him of making himself acquainted with how matters really did stand. 'Whenever you may feel inclined so to do, I shall be happy to hear from you that you have changed your view of the case.'[77] This, he did not do and brother and sister remained estranged for the rest of her life.

Adultery, separation and perjury were not the only scandals likely to drag the family name through the courts and press. As bad or worse to some minds was the threat of bankruptcy.

So it was that a bare four years after his final rejection by Emily and at the same time as his second marriage to Lady Mary and the beginning of his alienation from Lord Robert, Lord Salisbury became embroiled in the financial affairs of his cousin Viscount Ingestre. The story of his involvement is illustrative of his own financial astuteness, it also shows further aspects of his character: supportive and considerate, but uncompromising in the face of ineptitude and stupidity.

When his cousin, through repeated risky and failing ventures, was placed in a position likely to embarrass both him and his family, Salisbury, as a trustee of the Ingestre estates, stepped in and undertook a thorough audit of his affairs. 'I regret to say', he wrote to Lord Talbot, Ingestre's father, that the aspect of them is most unpromising. The assets are very few the liabilities very large'. It would appear that the trustees had borrowed money on Ingestre's behalf in order to pay debts and avoid bankruptcy, and that Salisbury himself was acting as guarantor.[78] In order to prevent further profligacy by his cousin, thereby increasing the debt still further, he arranged for the trustees to release payments not to Ingestre himself but to Lady Sarah, his wife. Lady Sarah's correspondence with her benefactor was touching in its expression of her heartfelt gratitude towards him. 'How can I tell you and Lord Mansfield (another trustee) all I feel to you both for all you have done for Ingestre'. She for her part had placed in the trustees' hands a detailed accounting of the family's household expenses, including the children's education, servants' wages, and rents on leased properties. Also laid bare were the details of the family income, including their respective marriage settlements.[79] By Salisbury's calculation, even after the proposed advances, Ingestre would still be living beyond his income to the tune of £1,500 per annum.[80]

Ingestre clearly felt it 'a bitter trial' having the allowance placed in his wife's hands[81], but felt compelled to express his 'sincere thanks to you and your co trustees for the trouble patience and anxiety you have been and are content to bestow on me and my affairs ... I am deeply sensible of all your kindness and of the considerate feeling which animates you'.[82] Much to the frustration of Salisbury, though, his cousin had clearly not learned his lesson where imprudent financial ventures were concerned. Just a few weeks later he was writing to Salisbury talking about a scheme for buying one or two hundred sheep from him.[83] My dear Ingestre, he replied, 'You really must not be angry with me if I join with Mansfield in giving you a most probationary epistle; but you really do not appear to me at all aware of the real state of your affairs'. Well this unhappy state of awareness could not be allowed to continue and the real state of his affairs was laid on the line with brutal frankness. 'You talk of buying one or two hundred sheep. You have not one or two hundred pence to pay for them.' Salisbury's own liability was enormous. 'My securities for you amount now to nearly £17,000. Mansfield has advanced you £17,600 on which account I am very much afraid he is in very great jeopardy ... and you talk of making purchases of farming stock'. He ended the missive with a heartfelt plea that Ingestre should not indulge the slightest hope that he could be relieved from his present embarrassments without enormous sacrifice. 'Do not think me harsh or unfeeling in writing you all this. It is written to help you for the sakes of your wife and children'.[84] To no avail. As Ingestre's dealings with a number of dubious associates began to unravel he wrote to Salisbury recklessly venturing the opinion that he had been foolish to guarantee money individually rather than through the trust. The reply was immediate and, this time, uncompromising. 'My dear Ingestre', he wrote, 'For Heaven's sake if you have any desire to get quit of your embarrassments do not meddle with your affairs'. While there are elements of black comedy to the current reader of the correspondence, the reality of Ingestre's situation was unquestionably dire, as Salisbury's blow by blow analysis of the financial situation showed.[85] Lady Sarah needed no persuading. 'What an unspeakable relief it would be to my mind if he would leave it to your arrangement and would not interfere himself.'[86] This, of course, was a vain hope and the beginning of 1847 saw Salisbury appealing to Lady Sarah's uncle, Lord John Beresford, Archbishop of Armagh, Primate of Ireland, for assistance. There had been a long standing quarrel between Ingestre and Lady Sarah's brothers following the death of her father, Henry Beresford, 2nd Marquess of Waterford, and an appeal against the terms of his will was making slow progress. On behalf of Ingestre and the trustees, Salisbury offered to drop the appeal in return for financial support,[87] but despite protestations of sympathy for the situation nothing changed.[88] By Autumn 1847, Lady Sarah was writing in despair to ask if 'anything ultimately is to be hoped, or done in the Chiny affair'; Chiny being an estate in Belgium in which her husband had invested.[89] The short answer was no, there was no hope and nothing to be done. But just over a year later, Lord Talbot died, and Ingestre inherited both the title and his father's fortune. Much of the latter was, if not squandered, expended upon an expensive legal battle in the House of Lords which resulted in 1860 in

Ingestre succeeding to the titles and estates of the Earls of Shrewsbury and Waterford. By this time, Lord Salisbury was nearing seventy years of age and was doubtless relieved to be rid of this particular family liability.

∞

In April 1847, amid the problems created by Lord Cranborne's health and Lord Robert's temperament, his estrangement from his sister Emily and the financial disasters of his cousin, Ingestre, Lord Salisbury embarked upon a second marriage to Lady Mary Catherine Sackville-West. Salisbury was by that time fifty-six years old, she a mere twenty three. Though, in the succeeding six years, Lady Mary bore him five children, three sons and two daughters, there was no doubt in anyone's mind that this really was a marriage of convenience. For him, Hatfield needed a hostess and his sons by Frances Mary needed the stabilising influence of a step-mother. For her, the marriage presented the opportunity not for social advancement but for social influence. Unlike Frances Mary, whose place in society rested solely upon that of her husband, Lady Mary came from an old and distinguished family. Her father, Lord De La Warr, had been Lord in Waiting to both George III and George IV, and his daughters had been childhood companions to the Princess Victoria at Kensington Palace.[90] As mistress of Hatfield she was able to attract 'distinguished spirits in every sphere'; these, including the Duc and Duchesse d'Aumale and Sophie, Queen of Holland, were 'received on the footing of intimate friends'. Then there were Lord Robert's Oxford contemporaries and the leading politicians of the day: Aberdeen, Palmerston,

Disraeli and Stanley; not forgetting the writers such as Edward Bulwer-Lytton and Charles Kingsley. Through the Salisbury family connections with Henry Wellesley, Lady Georgiana's step-son who followed his father into the Paris Embassy, she was presented to Napoleon III and listened to the leading French thinkers of the day.[91] And, of course, there was her friendship with the Duke of Wellington. For his part there was nothing extraordinary in this. As a member of the Cecil family through Georgiana's marriage to his younger brother, regular social intercourse was the norm. Through both the family and the political connection he had become a close friend of Salisbury and spent much time at Hatfield, just as the Salisburys were invited frequently to Stratfield Saye and Walmer. That he corresponded so assiduously with both of the Marchionesses in turn was also not surprising. Even before his doomed to fail marriage to Kitty Pakenham in 1806 he had gained a reputation as 'a ladies' man'. For their part, particularly after Waterloo, he was worshipped by a series of society women.[92] The diary of the 2nd Marchioness of Salisbury, Frances Mary, while at no time suggesting an affair with the Duke, shows an almost childlike desperation to be affirmed as a particular friend. 'He called me his friend, twice over, with emphasis, as if he would have said "my first and best friend", and expressed a confidence in me which I feel with a gratitude and pleasure I cannot express'.[93]

By the time of Salisbury's marriage to Lady Mary, Wellington was an old man in his late seventies and the tenor of his correspondence with her was less to do with the theatre and social occasions and more to do with major developments and events of the day and with political issues at home and abroad: the new railroads, the Crystal

Palace, the Civil List, the Queen's progress, the resignation of Palmerston, the Militia Bill, the General Haynau scandal, the Papal Brief of Pio Nono, the anti Orleanist policies of Louis Napoleon in France and much more.[94] Certainly she led a full and independent life in a manner unknown to her predecessor. It should be remembered though that the marriage of Lord Salisbury to Lady Mary coincided with his increased involvement in national affairs, which in addition to his responsibilities on his home and other estates meant that he was frequently absent from Hatfield. So it is hardly surprising that Lady Mary was left to bring up her children and to create her own social network with much less involvement from her husband than had been the case with his first family by Frances Mary. Sadly, of the more personal aspects of her family life there is little record, her journal having been destroyed. 'A few memoranda of conversations jotted down on half sheets of notepaper have alone survived.'[95]

Two years after Salisbury's death in 1868, Lady Mary married Edward Henry Stanley, 15th Earl of Derby. As Lord Stanley, he had been frequent visitor to Hatfield. He was said to have adored her and 'apart from his career as a statesman, in which she was absorbed, they shared a common love of literature and scenery'. It was a happy union which lasted until his death in 1893. She lived to see in the next century, dying in December 1900.[96]

⊱⊰

Lord Salisbury's last will made provision for both of his families. As heir to the Marquessate, Lord Robert inherited all of his father's personal estate other than that already disposed of in codicils. The settlement of the Salisbury family estates provided for at the time of his marriage to Frances Mary was effected as agreed. Lady Mildred and Lady Blanche had each received £10,000 on their respective marriages and were now advanced further sums of £20,000 each. Lord Eustace had received £5,000 in India stock on his marriage and £10,000 in East India Debentures. In accordance with another deed of 1857, he received a further sum of £220,000 on his father's death, and by codicil he also received River Lee Bonds or Securities for money under the seal of River Lee Navigation Corporation bearing dates prior to 1865. All of the Salisbury daughters received a further £500 by codicil. The Princes Meadow, in present day Lambeth, and Wenlock Basin, in present day Islington, both of which attracted a substantial income in rents and tolls, were left in trust to ensure the futures of all of the Sackville-West children. Lady Mary received the comparatively small cash sum of £5,000 together with the Bourne Plate[97], all wines spirits, linens and china at 20 Arlington Street, 2 carriages, 4 horses and all ponies.

Also remembered were those household servants who had given particular service: £1 per week for life for Lord Salisbury's steward; 15s a week for life for his valet; a year's wages for all servants in service at his death who had lived with him for twenty years or more; half a year's wages for servants in service at his death who had lived with him for fifteen years; £1 per week for his clerk of works; 10s a week for life for his bricklayer and to outdoor servants of 20 years or more, one year's wage. He requested that his heir, Viscount Cranborne, continue payment of the pensions he had been paying to some individuals for long and faithful services.[98]

Lord Salisbury's kindness in remembering those who had

served him faithfully was recognised in *The Hertford Mercury*, which reported in his obituary that 'he had many old servants and he never lost sight of or neglected them when they became too old to serve him. In his relations with them and with the humble people about his estate, he showed much kindness and even tender heartedness'. Of his family it was said that he 'was loved in his own house, and this is the highest tribute that can be borne to his character. His children regarded him with the affection which pride and caprice cannot inspire and his servants were devotedly attached to him'.[99]

2

---∞∞∞---

Hatfield: A Family Home

"My greatest happiness is being at Hatfield".[1] Lady Mildred's love of the ancestral home of the Cecils was a sentiment widely felt by family, friends and the many political associates who considered themselves privileged to gather there. As a child and then a young man, Lord Cranborne had been accustomed to the presence of the high society of Hatfield and Hertfordshire in his home. His mother, the 1st Marchioness, was renowned for the social gatherings which were the talk of the neighbourhood. Following in her footsteps, and in-keeping with his ultra conservative outlook on life, the 2nd Marquess, according to David Cecil, presided over a kind of 'regal, feudal open-house affair whose festive occasions were marked by huge gatherings where retainers and tenants were lavishly entertained with gallons of beer and specially slaughtered oxen, and the nobility and gentry with balls and banquets and garden parties'[2]. His first wife, Frances Mary, played hostess to such events at Hatfield while his second, Lady Mary, attracted a retinue from the political and literary elite of London and Europe.

David Cecil wrote of Hatfield that 'it was designed to be the house of a great nobleman'…yet 'the impression it leaves is not that of a palace; it is also a family home with the characteristics of a family home'[3]. Three generations earlier, Lord Salisbury had been a fierce protector of this family home, which he did much to improve and preserve; and when it was threatened he had fought tirelessly to preserve it.

Some of the improvements to the old house were necessitated by the great fire in which his mother died in 1835 and which destroyed the west wing. Characteristically, the changes he brought about here and elsewhere in the house took much of the interior back to the styles of the seventeenth century, with panelling and tapestries replacing the more elegant era of his parents. 'He gilded the Gallery ceiling, refashioned the Library and pretty well re-created the gardens.'[4]

In the Introduction to 'The Gardens at Hatfield', the present Dowager Marchioness, who was the prime mover behind the more recent renovations and improvements which visitors enjoy today, pays tribute to the work of the 2nd Marquess. 'With the accession of the second Marquess, in 1823, Hatfield was for the first time since the death of Robert Cecil (First Earl of Salisbury), in the care of an active and interested gardener. He restored the gardens round the house as he thought they had been when they were first created in Jacobean days. He made terraces on the east and west sides of the house...he laid out new parterres and a maze', and he built the brick openwork walls that surround some of the gardens.[5]

There was and still is, of course, much more than the house and garden at Hatfield, and Lord Salisbury was as protective of his Hertfordshire estates, which he considered to be an integral part of his home, as of the building.

Here, just as he found his way of life and most dearly held' beliefs threatened by industrial and social developments, the changes to infrastructure which supported economic growth threatened both his home and his neighbourhood. Canals, roads and railways all followed the old routes and Hatfield, straddling the Great North Road, inevitably became a focus for speculators. Salisbury was wise enough to know that he could not stop development altogether; furthermore, he had enough financial acumen to recognise the investment opportunities which infrastructural developments presented. His approach to the evident dichotomy of how to take advantage of opportunities and at the same time protect his home, estates and tenantry was to take control, a strategy played to perfection on his home ground where he wielded great influence.

The River Lee developments following from the Lee Navigation Improvement Act of 1850 did not impinge directly upon Salisbury's enjoyment of his home, though it was in his interest to ensure the safe passage of agricultural produce from his holdings near the course of the Lee. In any case, the issue of control was relatively simple. In 1844 he had become a Trustee of the River Lee Navigation, and in 1851 he became Chairman. The powers of the Trust had been strengthened under the Navigation Act of the previous year and were extended still further under the River Lea Water Act of 1855. It was recognised that under his 'able and vigorous management' the navigation was greatly improved: tonnage thereby increased, tolls reduced and income nearly doubled. The Royal Commission appointed to look into river pollution was so impressed with the huge progress made under his Chairmanship that they reported to Parliament that the work of the Trustees had proved a commercial success; 'a valuable convenience to towns on the banks and to districts inaccessible to railways'.[6] These improvements and the revenue which followed was, of course, extremely profitable for its shareholders. That the Salisbury finances benefited considerably is clear from the bequest of shares in the River Lee Corporation to be granted to Lord Eustace on his father's death, but set up as early as 1857.

Whilst working as a Trustee for the Lee Navigation and fully occupied with his Parliamentary and magisterial duties, the 1840s also saw Lord Salisbury taking on both the road and the railway companies in his determination to protect his Hatfield estates. The plans for changing the route of the Great North Road to accommodate railway development required concessions and permissions from him which in turn required planners and builders to involve him in each and every proposal. In the protracted negotiations he was shameless in using every advantage of his position and influence to get not just his own way but that of his tenants too.

From the outset of negotiations between Lord Salisbury and the North Road engineers, it was plain to see that he had no intention of giving ground in any way which would disadvantage his tenants or himself. But, clearly, agreement regarding the re-routing of the road had to be reached before plans for the railway could be completed and Salisbury could see advantages in moving forward as quickly as possible. There would be 'immediate employment for our poor and if the railroad will give us money we might begin as soon as the surveys are completed'[7] This was not to say that he encountered no opposition to his plans. One neighbour, Baron Dimsdale had got very short shrift when he complained of Salisbury's plan to move the existing turnpike road and have another made on the other side of Millwards Park. The public, he claimed would not in any way benefit by it, and 'many properties' including his own 'seriously injured' so that he was 'anxious to state (with every friendly and neighbourly feeling towards your Lordship) I am bound to give it my decided opposition'. In a cutting reply, Salisbury professed to be 'sorry to find that you were averse to any scheme for diminishing the nuisance of the railroad to those through whose property it is to pass'. He added his surprise 'that you as a friend to the establishment of a rail road through Hatfield should wish to drive Mr.Gaussen and myself into an active and zealous opposition to your company'.[8]

Nothing escaped his attention and his superior knowledge of the working of Parliamentary standing orders and the regulations regarding notices was used to effect in getting inevitable changes carried out to the advantage of his own agenda. Having accepted that railway construction would not be stopped and in anticipation of the financial incentives which would precede its commencement in return for access to his estate, he decided that a Bill, which would delay everything, would not be needed. Once that was out of the way, he was intent on pursuing the concerns of his tenants and the town, even drawing sketches of the proposed route to accompany his objections. The first objection was on behalf of a Mr Pryor, since the route would take the road through his garden and stables. 'I have endeavoured to make a sketch which I enclose which would avoid his premises by a branch at the point marked A. I do not think the expense would be greater, as there would be fewer buildings to take'. The second was the destruction of the pond which 'would leave no resource to the town of Hatfield in the case of fire. Would it be objected to by the railroad, to give a pond equal in extent between the railroad and road? ... the pond in question is furnished by an abundant spring'. The third was the issue of an 8ft embankment which was unsightly for Mr Faithfull as well as himself. They had been told that the ground would be raised on both sides to conceal it, but Mr Faithfull 'is not satisfied without your assurance to that effect.' Mr Faithfull was also concerned that he would have difficulty getting out of his gate. 'Would you have the kindness also to state that he would have a convenient bridge over the railroad which is there in deep cutting to the high road?'

Every complaint followed by a request for change was put forward with the utmost courtesy. There was no need for bluster. Lord Salisbury knew that the road agents and the Turnpike Trust would be unlikely to engender his ire and a likely end to cooperation by refusing. The reply is indicative of just how powerful he was once the negotiations were under his control. On behalf of the Company, Mr Giles assured him that 'it will afford me much satisfaction to carry out your Lordship's wishes as to the roads and pond... the embankment ...and the bridge'. The issue of Mr Pryor was more difficult, as it was found that there was no alternative to passing through his land. 'It seems therefore that we must negotiate with him ... perhaps you will have the kindness to let me know if you wish me to talk to Pryor. I shall not do so unless you desire it.'[9]

A similar scenario was played out between Salisbury and the railway companies. Here, though, the added incentive of possibly huge returns on investments came into play, which inevitably involved competition, underhand tactics, and parliamentary lobbying by the three contenders for the railway between London and York. He was drawn into the issue as early as early 1841, when proposals were made for an additional branch line to Hertford. Local interested parties were anxious to engage his support. The opponents of the line were doomed to disappointment for he appears to have taken it upon himself to assist in drafting the necessary Railway Bill for which he received the thanks of the proposers who expressed the view that 'it is universally acknowledged in Hertford that if we get the Railway here at all it is attributable to your Lordship's firmness and exertions in our favour'.[10]

The negotiations and behind the scenes endeavours were much more complex when it came to the main route. From summer 1841, Salisbury was locked in battle with the agents for the proposed London and York Direct Northern Railway regarding the route through Hatfield. In the summer of 1844 he was incensed to find that it had been put about that he was a consenting party to the projected railway. 'All I can at present state', he said in a counter statement, 'is that it is very unlikely that I should consent to increase tenfold the only existing nuisance in the shape of roads to my House at Hatfield, and from my knowledge of the country I presume that this would be the line your engineers will probably adopt'.[11] This was followed by an apology from Sir John Rennie, thenceforth the primary negotiator with Salisbury, who claimed distinctly to have understood that 'Your Lordship made no pledge either one way or another respecting the proposed … line'.

Asking for his help in setting up a meeting of the noblemen and gentlemen in the vicinity who would be affected by the scheme, he pledged to ensure that 'no use shall be made of Your Lordship's name without express authority and that no step shall be taken without previously acquainting Your Lordship'.[12] Further correspondence with Sir John Rennie and his colleague Mr Gravatt on the question of access to the estate continued for a further five months before Salisbury became aware that the chairman of one of the proposed lines to York, Mr Astell, was known to him. He was glad to find, he said, that in the difficult negotiations ahead he would be dealing with an old friend and one who would not unnecessarily impose upon his property.[13] In December 1844, he nevertheless felt compelled to seek advice from the Vice President of the Board of Trade regarding the rival schemes for a railway to York. Lord Dalhousie was clearly in no doubt that Salisbury's enquiry was not for the purpose of obstruction but in order to gain assurances about the route through Hatfield. 'It would at all times give me great pleasure to be of use to you', he replied, 'especially under circumstances in which your comfort and the enjoyment of your residence appear to be so deeply involved'. He confirmed that there were three companies applying for Bills to form a railway to York: '1. Hudson's line from Cambridge to Lincoln. 2. The Direct Northern. 3. The London and York. To Hudson's line you have no personal objection. But to the other two you have one and the same objection…that they injure your property and destroy the privacy of your residence.' The advice did not end there, though, and Salisbury was left in no uncertainty about the course of action expected of him. 'I am very clearly of the opinion that having told the two companies in the first instance that if they would obviate your objections to the course of their line then you would not oppose them in Parliament; and the Direct Northern having agreed to adopt your line and still continuing to declare themselves willing to adopt your line; you cannot, as a man of honour, join the London and York, since the joining them would virtually be to oppose the Direct Northern, which you have promised not to do on certain conditions, which conditions they have religiously fulfilled.'[14]

However Salisbury felt about having his honour possibly called into question it did not prevent him from taking vigorous action against perceived breaches of agreements to allow access to surveyors. Claims and counter claims of the London and York Company and its rivals continued to blight relationships and impede progress and, eventually, completely out of patience, Salisbury again wrote to Lord Dalhousie, now President of the Board of Trade, with a proposed House of Lords standing order concerning trespass by railway surveyors. His argument was that the existing 'law of trespass is quite insufficient to protect the owner or occupier of property from its invasion by any speculating engineer'. Worse, 'he must resort for protection to violence'. The letter ended in true Salisbury overstatement with the warning that 'the evil which I wish to remedy is daily increasing and will I have no doubt lead to personal conflicts and perhaps to bloodshed'. Dalhousie, having received a similar missive on the same subject pledged to draw it to the attention of the Railway Committee of the House of Lords at their first meeting.[15]

Four months later, the London and York Bill finally received Royal Assent as the Great Northern Railway Act.

The Railway was not to pass through Hatfield Park, but there were still issues Salisbury felt compelled to deal with; the proposed refreshment rooms and railway station at Hatfield; still the issue was his home. 'I rather unwillingly acceded,' he wrote to the new railway company, 'to a proposal for altering the station upon terms which certainly held out pecuniary advantages to me, but I stated that I would not part with the frontage to the high road. My reasons for this reservation were that parting with it would enable you to erect an hotel or houses which would be a great annoyance to my view and would be dangerous rivals to my two inns.'[16] As ever Lord Salisbury was appeased and terms were agreed which protected both his view and his inns.

With the newly routed North Road and the arrival of the railway, the old town of Bishop's Hatfield was altered irrevocably. The census returns from 1841 to 1871 show how the more genteel occupiers of the old streets adjoining the grounds of Hatfield House, now by-passed and no longer serving a privileged passing clientele from the old coaching route, either drifted away or were forced to diversify. Whether Lord Salisbury recognised the effect of the changes in his immediate neighbourhood is unclear, but he achieved his wish to retain the peace and comfort of his home, which today is bordered by modern roads but is distinctly separate from the new town of Hatfield.

With the permission of the 7th Marquess of Salisbury from the
collection at Hatfield House:

Hatfield House: Sketch of West Garden and West Wing after the 1835 fire
(P1110552)

Watercolour of Hatfield House North Front, 1844 (00584)

Drawing of Hatfield gardens in 1851, peopled with Jacobean figures
(P1110552)

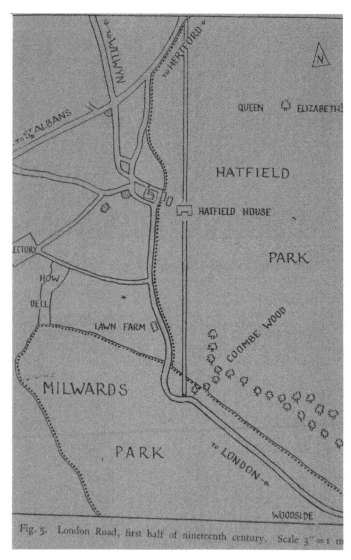

Fig. 5. London Road, first half of nineteenth century. Scale 3″ = 1 m

Maps of Hatfield Park before and after the building of the railway: from
Hatfield and its People, Book 1, 1959, pages 8 and 9.
(00576 & 00577)

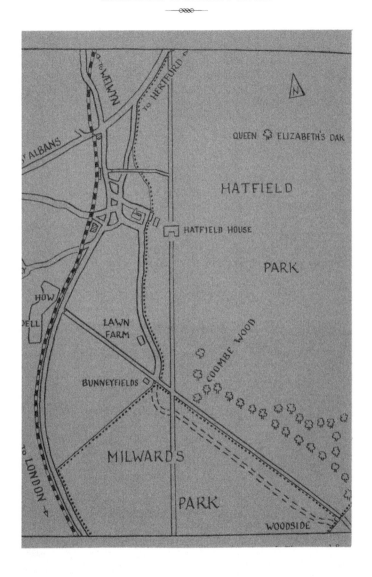

The 2nd Marquess of Salisbury: print of the portrait painted for the
Middlesex magistrates, 1854 (P1110548)

The Queen's Visit to Hatfield: print in the *Illustrated London News, 1846*
(P1110563)

The Queen's Visit to Hatfield, 1846:
Ball in the Long Gallery (1110561)

Supper in the Marble Hall (1110562)

Judging by the deference accorded him by powerful capitalist interests, the extent of the 2nd Marquess's influence in his home county extended much beyond that derived purely from his name and estates. In every important sphere of activity in Hertfordshire and in neighbouring counties he accrued titles and powers which he was shameless in using to promote and enforce his will; though this was always within the letter and upholding of the law.

As Chairman of the Herts Quarter Sessions from December 1841, he held significant judicial, civil and administrative powers. As well as hearing, with a jury, cases referred from the magistrates courts, he was nominally responsible for roads, bridges, policing, gaols, asylums, licensing of public houses, county rates and, on behalf of the Lord Lieutenant of the County, the county militia. He at first claimed that he had insufficient time to take on the responsibility because of his other commitments, [17] but soon bowed to the pressure of a unanimous vote by his peers.[18] In reality, much of the work involved, beyond sitting in court, was handled by the county Clerk of the Peace who was, in turn, assisted by qualified solicitors. This was probably as well, since he had only recently been approached by Peel to accept the Lord Lieutenancy of the County of Middlesex, a position of greater social influence than that of Hertfordshire.

As Lord Lieutenant of Middlesex between 1841 and his death in 1868 Salisbury wielded still further power at a local level. The Militia Act of 1662 had made the Lieutenant responsible for the county militia and from 1757 gave him the authority to assemble, arm and command it. While the need for a local militia had receded somewhat in the early eighteenth century, the threat of invasion during the

Napoleonic Wars and the period of domestic unrest in the 1800s had emphasised its importance once again. In 1854, the Militia Act enabled the Government to embody the militia in the event of war with a foreign country, thus heightening its significance and that of the county officials responsible for Militia Muster Rolls and commissions.[19]

The militia had, of course, been of great importance to Salisbury even before his accession to the marquessate. Having been thwarted in his wish to enter the army, because of his perceived responsibilities as heir to the Hatfield estates, and having failed to persuade Wellington to take him with him to Paris, he had sought some kind of consolation in his role as Colonel of the Herts Militia and Major of the Herts Yeomanry Cavalry. So it was an occasion of great pride when, in 1846, Queen Victoria and Prince Albert paid a visit to Hertfordshire, and he was told by George Anson, groom of the bedchamber to Prince Albert, that 'The Queen will be very glad to accept the services of your Hertfordshire Yeomanry on Her Majesty's entrance into the County'.[20]

The decade between 1841 and 1851 was a time of significant achievement for Lord Salisbury: Lord Lieutenant of Middlesex; Chairman of the Herts Quarter Sessions; Trustee and then Chairman of the River Lee Navigation; marriage to Lady Mary Catherine Sackville-West. But it was, undoubtedly, the visit of the Queen to Hatfield in 1846 which brought him the greatest personal satisfaction, for he was not just asked to usher Her Majesty into the county, he was invited to entertain her for a full two days in his beautiful home. What is more, he was given permission to demonstrate his favour with Her Majesty in true Hatfield style. 'The Queen', wrote Anson, 'has no objection to a ball taking place … and would on no account deprive you of the pleasure of gratifying your county neighbours'. 'The Queen and Prince', he added, 'like always to breakfast alone; luncheon they generally have with the general company.' As for the accommodation, 'Pray do not fear that you can go wrong as to the furniture of Her Majesty's apartment. Her Majesty's taste is quite simple and H M allows me to suggest nothing on this score, being assured that everything will meet her full approval.'[21] Not to recognise the greatness of the occasion with suitable renovations at Hatfield was, of course, unthinkable and, redecorated in red and gold for the occasion, the royal apartment remains as a testament to one of the great highlights of Lord Salisbury's life.

Today, the 2nd Marquess's portrait hangs in the Armoury of Hatfield House beside that of his first wife, Frances Mary. Elsewhere in the House are the portraits of the five generations of Gascoyne-Cecils who have followed him and have in turn made their own mark on the house and grounds. The lasting beauty that they, like the 2nd Marquess, have sought to protect and preserve is summarised simply in the words of Lord Salisbury himself, and quoted by David Cecil his great grandson in his book *The Cecils of Hatfield House*: 'There is not a more perfect place in all England'.[22]

3

A True English Nobleman

Lord Salisbury's obituary in *The Times* summarised most eloquently the position which he held by virtue of his birth, his inheritance and his talent. 'Lord Salisbury's great wealth placed him in a foremost position in the political sphere and his character increased the influence of his large possessions'... 'His honours were such as must always fall to a man of his position who possesses taste for public life. There are certain peers', though, 'who are almost by inheritance knights of our most famous Order, if they are in any degree careful to discharge the duties of their station ... 'Lord Salisbury was such a peer.[1] *The Hertford Mercury* listed those honours: Lord Lieutenant of the county of Middlesex, Deputy Lieutenant of Argyllshire, Knight of the Garter, Colonel of the Herts Militia and Major of the South Herts Yeomanry Cavalry, Chairman of the Herts Quarter Sessions, Chairman of the Board of Guardians of the Hatfield Union and Chairman of the River Lee Navigation. He took office in the Earl of Derby's first two administrations, as Lord Privy Seal and then as Lord President of the Council.[2] As for 'the large possessions', in addition to the immediate Hatfield estate, he held extensive properties in Dorset, Essex, Bedfordshire,

London and Middlesex, and in Liverpool. From the mid 1840's he also held ownership of the Island of Rum.

Frances Mary, in her diary[3], and Lady Mary in letters to Wellington[4], made reference to Salisbury's travels to Lancashire, Dorset, and Rum, and his own correspondence with his officials in each of these places shows how closely he controlled the management of all his estates. It would not have been in keeping with his character to have played the role of absentee landlord; indeed, he ran Rum very much as his own little kingdom. Lady Gwendolen Cecil wrote of her grandfather that 'he had a dominating sense of public duty and an unhesitating readiness to accept responsibility in the performance of it'. While 'he claimed the rights of government', she said, 'he unreservedly accepted its burdens. Where his poorer neighbours were concerned, while his methods were autocratic, his aims were purely altruistic'.[5] As *The Standard* said of him, 'he was in all respects the pattern of a true English nobleman'[6].

But what was the pattern of a true English nobleman? In the eighteenth century of Salisbury's youth, the pattern had been driven by a model of paternalism owing more to a feudal economy and social arrangements than to the modern urban capitalism of Victorian Britain. In the years following the revolution in France, though, the need to formalise the inbred and instinctive roles of the landed classes in England, led to 'a wave of paternalistic writings that crested between 1827 and 1847'[7]. First and foremost was Edmund Burke's *Reflections on the Revolution in France*, which affirmed and gave strength to the growth of social and political conservatism, which was in part a reaction to the Napoleonic wars and in part to the social and economic upheavals wrought by encroaching industrialism.

It cannot be said with certainty that the 2nd Marquess read or was influenced by such writings, though Burke's *Reflections* are known to have been circulated widely amongst the conservative political classes and the 1790 edition is still to be found in the library at Hatfield. Judging by Salisbury's known actions and attitudes, Burke's emphasis on the importance of property and hierarchy, and the description of the rich 'as trustees for those who labour for them' and the guarantors of 'those connections, natural and civil, that regulate and hold together the community of subordination'[8,] are likely to have struck a chord.

Other texts of the period, are catalogued and still present at Hatfield: M. Sadler's *Ireland; its evils and their remedies* (1829), W. Sewell's *Christian Politics* (1844) and a complete run of *The Quarterly Review,* from 1809. *The Quarterly Review*, consistently in opposition to religious movements such as Unitarianism which threatened the supremacy of the Anglican Churches, and radicalism, which threatened the stability of the old political order, would certainly have reflected and fed the fears of many of Lord Salisbury's class. Sadler and Sewell both described a social and political system within which the ownership of property, social control and benevolence was paramount; a system which 'fitted the English landlord's daily experiences as proprietor, magistrate and neighbour and fitted also his jealous regard for his autonomy and his hatred of the central government'[9]. But, while Lord Salisbury was a most assiduous guardian of his autonomy, he was throughout his public life an enthusiastic parliamentarian who actively sought ministerial office in successive governments. While he would doubtless have agreed with Sewell's and other writers' call for 'a government that would suppress seditious writings, close down libellous presses, punish criminals severely, repress disorderly meetings, and penalise dissent'[10] he was not a supporter of capital punishment[11].

So, Salisbury was not quite the model of the old paternalistic order, but he was even less a supporter of the emerging modern model of writers such as Chalmers and Coleridge who sought to assimilate into a new paternalist philosophy acceptance of the laissez faire economy, the growth of manufactures, the practice of philanthropy and the promotion of self help.[12] He was above all an individualist, certain of his opinions and unwavering in his support of his church, his class and his party, and it was the attack upon all three of these anchors during the eighteen twenties, thirties and forties which saw him lost in a society where deferential bonds were breaking down and where money rather than lineage were coming to rule the day.

The first assault upon his cherished beliefs came not from the radical left but from his own party. The fact that on the issue of Catholic Emancipation he found himself forced into opposition against his political leader, his friend and his mentor, the Duke of Wellington, must have been a particularly bitter blow. Wellington, just as much as Salisbury, was a staunch opponent of Catholic Emancipation, but he was at the same time a realist who understood that, at the end of the day, Ireland had to be governed and O'Connell's victory in the Clare by-election meant that it would become ungovernable unless Emancipation were granted. He also understood that this was something which he could not achieve from his position as Prime Minister from the Lords. Like it or not, he was dependent upon strong leadership in the Commons and that could only come from his Home Secretary, Robert Peel.[13] When Peel finally saw the Emancipation Bill through the Commons in March 1829 he made an impassioned plea for expediency over party refusal to move with changed circumstances. To 'concede nothing to agitation' he said, 'is the ready cry of those who are not responsible – the vigour of whose decisions is often proportionate to their own personal immunity from danger, and to their imperfect knowledge of the true state of affairs'[14]. To Salisbury and his fellow Ultra Tories in the Lords this was not just a slur upon their intelligence and integrity but a damning betrayal of the Protestant establishment and therefore also of the sovereign as head of the church.

During the weeks of bitter debate on the Bill before its final reading in the Lords, he wrote to Wellington 'that it is with great pain that I differ from you on any and much more on a question of this importance. I could not conscientiously follow any other line of conduct'[15]. The rift with Wellington was soon mended, but Peel was, until his death in July 1850, neither to be liked nor trusted by Salisbury. What is more, it was as a direct consequence of the Emancipation issue that the next and direst threat to the survival of his class gathered momentum.

The threat of revolution had for the past thirty years held together a society which was changing irrevocably, and the years between 1815 and 1820 saw a series of radical organisations, risings and plots: the Hampden Clubs, the Political Union societies, the mass meetings in Spa Fields and St Peter's Fields, the Cato Street Conspiracy and the

Blanketeers' march. In 1819 Wellington was forced to inform the Cabinet that 'a reduced and scattered army now of only 65,000 home-based men could not effectively interpose itself against a concentrated rebellious outbreak'[16]. As if this were not enough, the radical movement was gaining ground through the growth of the press in provincial manufacturing towns. *The Leeds Mercury, The Sheffield Independent* and *The Manchester Guardian* attracted a huge circulation amongst the radical free-trade middle classes, while cheap papers such as Cobbett's *Political Register* found a wide readership amongst the journeymen and labourers. Taken together with the vitriolic cartoons of George Cruikshank and the political caricatures of William Hone, the established radical line 'that the distress of the people was caused by corruption in high places and by the misgovernment of a largely unelected elite'[17] had by the mid twenties become widespread and to those of Salisbury's mind extremely dangerous. Suppression through the suspension of Habeas Corpus, granting powers to magistrates for the control of public meetings, the introduction of a punitive duty on newspapers and the strengthening of laws against seditious or libellous publications reduced the overt threat of revolution, but the demand for reform was not going away. All that was needed was a catalyst and, indirectly, Emancipation created just such an opportunity for the radicals, whose ranks were being swelled by the call for reform by substantial numbers of the middle class.

The challenge precipitated by Emancipation was that it 'had shown that change was possible without revolution' and 'could be forced on Parliament by outside pressure'.[18] Already fired up about electoral abuses and corruption, it was the insistence of the Liberal Tories led by Huskisson that the boroughs of Penryn and East Retford should be disenfranchised, which led to their defection from the government and to the Clare by-election which brought the Emancipation issue to a head. It also split the anti reformers, led to the fall of Wellington's government and ushered in the Whigs and the Liberal Tories, united under the banner of reform and led by Earl Grey.

Months before Lord John Russell introduced the first of three Reform Bills into the Commons in March 1831, MPs and Lords were confronted with the reality of high bread prices following the failed harvest of 1829, the resulting distress and revolt of agricultural labourers across the South and East of England and the growth of the political unions: the General Political Union between the Lower and the Middle Classes of the People and the National Union of the Working Classes, which agitated for complete male suffrage.[19] Alarm amongst the landed classes was widespread and when a local county meeting for the reform of Parliament was organised by Whigs and moderate reformers in Hertford, Salisbury approached the issue as though the country was at war. Writing to Wellington in January 1831, he sought approval for a strategy to disengage the moderates. 'I could raise a storm about their ears', he said, 'by explaining to the voters that reform in Parliament means that they are to be disenfranchised and the right of voting given to persons rated to a certain extent. If I succeeded in this, there would be an end of all reform meetings in the county of Hertford and the same tactics would probably be adopted in many other places where there is powerful influence'. The risk he would run by doing this, though, was 'that a universal suffrage petition might be carried instead of one for moderate reform'.

Wellington's reply that he had not much experience of country meetings and preferred 'not to meddle with them'[20] was not encouraging, and less than two months later the field of combat moved to Westminster.

When the first Bill was unveiled, it did nothing to allay the fears of any but the already defected Tories. The proposal to reduce the number of borough seats and transfer them to the more populous towns, to increase the county representation relative to population and to give £10 renters the vote, passed the Second Reading in the Commons by just one vote. Grey, seeing the writing on the wall when an amendment was proposed which would certainly be defeated, went for dissolution, trusting to better his position in the subsequent election which was to 'become a virtual plebiscite for reform'[21]. The mood of the people was clear, and only 6 of the 34 MPs who had voted against the Second Reading were re-elected. When the second Reform Bill was brought up from the Commons to the Lords in October, with little changed, it was again rejected. The country went into a frenzy of protest and early rumours of Grey's approach to the King to create enough new peers to outvote the Ultras did little to calm matters. The resisters were not prepared to give way, though. For them the stakes were just too high. In May, Wellington had summarised their feelings and their fears most forcefully in a letter to Lady Salisbury. 'The truth', he said, 'is that the Union of the King, the Whigs, the Dissenters, the radicals, and the mob forms a monster too strong for anything excepting destruction.'[22] In the January following the second rejection, he wrote to Lord Strangford the opinion that 'there are two very easy and straight roads for the destruction of the British Monarchy. One is a moderate Reform Bill, as efficient as that thrown out last October by the House of Lords ... the other is to destroy even the semblance of independence in the House of Lords by creating Peers to counterbalance the majority which voted against the Reform Bill'.[23]

As the senior member of the aristocracy in Hertfordshire, Lord Salisbury became the focus for resistance and received numerous letters from notable Herts personages, mostly from the magistracy, in response to the address which he was to make on their behalf in an audience with the King. One recalled the state of France, and the 'similarity of the politics of this country at the present time', another wrote of a 'measure so pregnant with evil and so subversive of the principles of the constitution'. Others were not so certain, and noted an apathy on the subject 'amongst the yeomen and farmers whose interests' would 'be most materially affected by the measure of Reform'. [24] Salisbury, himself, entertained no such doubts and, when the King told him that 'many of his most loyal subjects had been prevented from expressing their opinions by the fear of the political unions', but that he had taken measures to allay such fears, he replied that 'the more violent of their opponents began to form contrary associations'. He later informed Wellington, that at this the King 'opened his eyes very wide'. He refrained, though, he said, from pointing out to the King 'that with the example of Ireland before him what must be the consequence of such a state of things'[25].

Salisbury worried later that he 'had rather gone too far' but he clearly felt no such restraint when addressing the Lords as the Reform Bill made its way through Parliament. By early 1832, increasing numbers of MPs and peers were of the view that a further rejection of the Bill would precipitate revolution and, in April, the Lords approached the Second Reading in some trepidation. Lord Salisbury was moved to admit 'that a very strong feeling did exist for some degree of reform, and, anti-reformer as he trusted he ever should remain, he confessed that he would be most willing to grant reform, and thereby meet the wishes of the people, if he thought he could do so consistently with security to the institutions of his country'. In particular, he questioned how 'security for any consistent line of policy in the Government be obtained, when in the event of a dissolution of Parliament, each Minister must depend upon the caprice of public opinion, consequent probably on the excitement of a general election, for his return to Parliament'[26]. Despite his pleas and those of nearly half of the House, the Second Reading was passed by nine votes. An amendment carried by Lord Lyndhurst, designed to delay discussion of the disenfranchisement of the rotten boroughs and therefore the whole Bill, led to a bizarre juggling of political possibilities for getting around the difficulty. Should the King create the necessary additional peers to carry the measure through as it stood? Should, or could, Wellington return to form a government to pass a moderate Reform Bill? Would Peel support Wellington in such a government, or not? In the event, the answer to all was no, Grey returned, and the Lords went into Committee once more. On the Third Day, Salisbury rose to declare that 'on the heads of the authors and supporters of the Bill would rest all the evil that would result from it, and he prayed God to grant that that evil might not be so great as he apprehended'[27]. At the Report stage, on 1 June, he moved an amendment in a last ditch attempt to preserve the rights of existing electors in boroughs to be disenfranchised, but he failed.[28] On 4 June, the Parliamentary Reform Bill for England passed the Third Reading, only 22 peers voting against. Lord Salisbury did not vote, he was not present.[29]

So, by the summer of 1832, Salisbury had witnessed and vigorously challenged the assaults upon the Anglican Establishment and upon the parliamentary supremacy of his class. The next and final assault upon his world had already been set in motion. It was to find a clear voice in 1834 at Tamworth and was finally to destroy the existence of the party to which he was committed with the Repeal of the Corn Laws in 1846.

Already reviled by many of his party following Catholic Emancipation, Sir Robert Peel had been reluctant to be seen once more as the great defector by supporting Wellington's bid to form a government of moderate reform. But within months of the Reform Bill's victory it became clear that Parliamentary reform was just the beginning of a fundamental shift in the domestic balance of power. Change was inevitable and the Tories had either to accept this or be annihilated. Indeed they nearly were in the December election which returned only 175 Tories against 483 Whigs. Peel's strategy for reversing this situation was to accept that some accommodation between the interests of the landowning class and those of commercial and industrial interests was the best defence against increasing radicalism. When Melbourne was forced to resign in November 1834, leaving Wellington in charge of a two month caretaker government, he returned from travelling in Italy to fight an election at Tamworth. In the now famous Manifesto, he pledged to carry out 'a careful review of institutions, civil and ecclesiastical ... combining with the firm maintenance of established rights, the correction of proved abuses and the redress of real grievances'[30]. This Lord Salisbury did not wish to hear. What was more, Peel, having assumed the premiership and de facto leadership of the party in December, was unable to form a majority in the Commons and, to the chagrin of Salisbury and Wellington, resigned, just four months later. As the ensuing drama unfolded, Frances Mary recorded in her diary, that she had never seen her husband so annoyed and that Wellington had gone to Peel's house and 'had a terrible scene' with him.[31]

By this time the antipathy sown during the Emancipation crisis ran deep, and was certainly encouraged by Frances Mary. She recorded, in detail, the reaction when four days after assuming office as Prime Minister the previous December, 'a messenger arrived from Peel offering Lord Salisbury the place of Master of the Horse'. But, he 'had long made up his mind to refuse a Household office; his wish is a place of business, and both with a view to his own future political career, and to the service of the cause to which, in this county especially, the acceptance of a sinecure would disable him from contributing, he determined to decline the offer'.[32] In February, she wrote a scathing account of Peel's conversation when she sat next to him at a dinner party. 'He then went on telling me to my infinite entertainment of the successful flattery he had employed in the various transactions and negotiations about offices'. "I never yet found the amount of flattery too large for any man to swallow", she reported Peel as saying. What was more, 'he had wrapped up the offer of the Buckhounds', an office which he had previously offered to Lord Wilton, who had refused it, 'by terming it "high office in connection with the personal service of the King"'. These, she said, were 'the very words Peel had used in his letter to

Lord Salisbury, all which he appeared to have forgotten'.[33] But Salisbury neither forgot nor forgave. On Peel's resignation on 10 April, he told his wife that 'there is something wanting in that man – it is very curious – with honesty and talents, and ability – still he is not a really great man'.[34]

Nevertheless, and no doubt reluctantly, he would have been bound to admit that Peel's approach boosted support for the new Conservatives, such that by the July 1841 election the new grouping was well placed to take control, winning 367 seats against the Whig Liberal Coalition's 291. Unhappily for Salisbury and his grouping in the Lords, though, the Conservative Party was also well placed to launch the final assault on old Tory interests.

The Corn Law, enacted in the final stages of the war with France to protect agricultural interests, had been eroded bit by bit since the early 20s, and by 1828 a sliding scale of duties had been introduced. But this did little to appease working men and manufacturers who saw 'a landowners' Parliament interfering with a free market in their narrow interest'[35], and ten years later the Anti-Corn Law League was founded by Manchester businessmen. When Peel resumed office as Prime Minister in 1841, he recognised that more must be done if a coalition between the Anti-Corn Law League and the rising Chartist movement were not to destroy all the gains made thus far. In his budget of 1842, he introduced tariff reductions, offset by the introduction of income tax, but the opposition continued to grow. For those old Tories who had fought the election of '41 'on the false prospectus of staunch support for agricultural protection'[36] he appeared duplicitous. When his 1845 budget moved still further in the direction of complete free trade they considered it to be a complete betrayal.

Salisbury might be excused a degree of Schadenfreude since he had been fighting a rearguard action ever since Peel's true intentions had been revealed in the '42 budget. Even before Peel introduced the Corn Bill to the Commons, Salisbury had written to him with a paper on the rate of corn duties. He recommended a suggestion made by one of his local farmers, which did not completely reject any reduction in duties, but argued that all corn duties during August and September should remain the same as the duties of the last levies in July and thereby prevent fraudulent rises in the price of corn. His additional comment that the latter was to his mind 'the only defect as a protection measure in the present corn law'[37], placed him firmly in the protectionist camp, and his opinions, therefore, of no consequence. When, the following year, he attempted to induce Wellington to present his view that the wages of the manufacturers were not affected by the price of corn and that the wages of the agricultural labourer were regulated by the price, Wellington was not prepared to intervene and urged him to talk directly to Peel.[38]

By December of 1845, opposition to Peel, had mounted and not just on the question of duties. He was now pursuing policies to build the loyalty of the Irish middle class by introducing complete equality for the Catholics. When he decided to treble the grant to the Catholic seminary at Maynooth and make it a permanent charge on the Exchequer, the Protectionists joined with the Anglicans and the fall of Peel seemed imminent.[39]

The debates on the Corn Laws demonstrated the extent to which the Tories within the Conservative grouping felt angered and betrayed, and the correspondence between

Salisbury and one of his staunchest allies in Hertfordshire, Granville Ryder, revealed the depth of his despair about public life at this point. In the expectation of a general election, the selection of a candidate for Hertford was crucially important, but this was not an easy matter. In a reply to Ryder on the question of possible candidates, Salisbury declared that 'I never felt so completely despondent upon politics in general and more especially upon those of this County as I do at the present moment. … We have neither men, money nor machinery to embark upon the contest which must follow.' He ended the letter on a note of utter despair. 'As far as I am concerned, I am soured and embittered … to a degree I can hardly express. Humble as my political life has been, I have steadily adhered to one line of politics which has been represented by one set of men. I have sacrificed my time and I may say a considerable fortune to the [? support] of my opinions.' Referring to Wellington, he felt sure that he would 'withdraw himself from any parliamentary warfare' and 'even if he did not his age renders it unlikely that he should be able to continue it for any length of time. I stand quite alone'.[40]

Ryder's reply of 20th December sympathised with Salisbury's despair and paid tribute to his efforts on behalf of Conservatism. 'Few persons have done so much as you have done for the great cause of Conservatism or have done it so heartily and so well'.[41]

At the end of the year, Lord John Russell failed to form a government and Peel resumed office. Peel's Secretary for the Board of Control, Viscount Mahon, who owed his Commons seat for the borough of Herford to Lord Salisbury's influence, wrote to Salisbury in early February explaining why he had not resigned as had many other Tory stalwarts. He also informed him that it was expected that the Bill to repeal the Corn Law would pass the Commons by 'not less than one hundred and twenty majority'. It may have been some consolation that he could not 'think it in the least probable that Sir Robert should stand very much longer as Minister, so strong is the feeling against him.'[42]

But the awaited fall was not to come yet, for Peel was able to take advantage of the famine in Ireland to get his way in Commons and Lords. So far as Salisbury was concerned there was no just ground[43], and once again he was at odds with Wellington. The Duke also questioned the extent of the famine, but recognised the 'difficulty founded upon the social habits of nearly the whole of the lower class of the Irish population in raising each for his own family the provisions which it should consume.' He also condemned the practice of labour mortgaged against rent, which left little possibility of families paying for food. But still a realist, he saw that if Russell could not form a government and Peel would not, unless he was able to continue on the path to free trade, the real issue was not 'what the corn law should be? But whether the Queen should have a Government.' Feeling 'then bound to stand by the Sovereign', he urged Salisbury to take a course upon this occasion which will be worthy of your station, your talents and patriotism.'[44] Salisbury was not to be swayed. In a bitterly critical letter to Wellington following Peel's speech on the subject in the House of Commons, he referred to 'the chivalrous devotion with which you have sacrificed your judgment for the support of the Queen's Government'. Were he to relinquish his independence of conscience he continued, 'it would not be to your superior judgment, experience and known character; for nobleness of purpose and integrity; but to the vacillating policy of Sir Robert Peel.'[45]

As the inevitable repeal bill made its way through Parliament, Salisbury's bitterness against the man who had seemed to have set out systematically to destroy his world came to a head. In a most revealing letter to Ryder in late May, he laid bare the reasons for the antipathy bordering on loathing which he felt for Peel. 'I have come to the deliberate opinion that a party of which Sir Robert Peel is the head is not a party to which I can belong. I am reduced to the alternative of either believing him to be dishonest, which I do not, or of thinking that pressure from without is the sole motive of his actions.' The only course of action open to those of his opinion, he felt, was to 'draw a marked distinction between Peel and the rest of the cabinet and to use every effort to force him individually to resign'. He saw 'no other possibility of preventing the accession of the Whigs to office. And I must candidly confess that I should prefer even this to the continuance of Peel'.[46] He was to get both. At the beginning of July, he was gratified to be able to write to Ryder with the news that Peel had been expelled from office and that the reins of Tory/Conservative leadership had passed to Lord Stanley.[47] But there was a heavy price to pay: virtual obscurity for the Tory wing of a shattered Conservative party and nearly six years of Whig government under Lord John Russell. 'Altogether the future looked dark,' wrote David Cecil. 'Every morning he would open the newspaper and say "It is all very bad. Depend on it the end of the world is coming".'[48]

❧

Personal tragedy was no stranger to Lord Salisbury. He had endured the death of his beloved first wife in 1839 and, at the time of Peel's fall, was still enduring the tragedy of his eldest son. A personal tragedy of another kind was Salisbury's inability to rate his own worth other than in terms of national political appointment.

As early as 1814, he had begged Wellington to take him to Paris as attaché to his embassy, [49] but was disappointed to learn that Wellington, having written to his mother, had 'received two letters from her in which she expresses in such strong terms her disinclination and that of Lord Salisbury … that I cannot but recommend it to you to give it up.'[50] He must have been disappointed again when Wellington failed to find a position for him in his cabinet of 1828. By 1834, he was an experienced member of the House of Lords who wielded significant influence among the Tory aristocracy and he was deeply angered by Peel's derisory offer of a household sinecure. Having been overlooked once more in 1841, he wrote to Wellington of his deep frustration and to sound him out about a step up in the peerage to a dukedom. 'For near thirty years that I have been in Parliament,' he wrote, 'I have followed the same view of politics with yourself. During that time I have received no mark of favour from the Crown … I have sacrificed on all occasions the claims which I imagined I possessed to employment that I might not in the slightest degree embarrass the leaders of the party'. Unfortunately, Wellington's reaction was, again, not encouraging. If his friend persisted in asking him to intercede on his behalf he would do so, but he made it clear that he would expect Peel to 'consider nothing on making up his decision upon the application, excepting his duty'. Salisbury was quick to retract his request, and assured the Duke that as far as he was concerned 'honours (unless I could obtain them by services) have never had very great charms ... the object I have sighed after all my life from the time when I asked you to take me as an attaché to Vienna to the present has been employment'.[51]

Three months later, in December 1841, and despite Wellington's lack of support and Salisbury's lack of enthusiasm for honours, Peel wrote to him offering the Lord Lieutenancy of Middlesex. The honour, which considerably increased his influence in local affairs and which he held until his death, was in the gift of the Queen; but the fact that it was awarded on the Prime Minister's recommendation no doubt lessened his satisfaction in the preferment. In March of the following year he was obliged to write to Peel again to thank him for the award of Knight of the Garter, but it was another year before he could bring himself to appeal directly to Peel for employment and not until April 1844 did he make a direct appeal for a specific appointment. Asking Peel to recall the request he had made the previous year he spoke of his 'anxiety of employment in almost any public capacity'. He had heard that Lord Lonsdale intended to resign the Post Office and would 'esteem it a great obligation if you would confer it upon me'. He reminded Peel that his father had held the same office and hoped that this would 'afford some inducement to you to view my present application in a favourable light'. Poor Lord Salisbury did not have to wait long for the result of his request. Peel responded on the same day with the crushing reply that, firstly, he had no reason to think that Lord Lonsdale was contemplating retirement and that, in any case, 'the rule on which I have invariably acted since my accession to office, and on to which I should wish for the sake of the public interests inflexibly to adhere, is to fetter myself by no engagements whatever, or assurances however vague or qualified, in respect to the nomination to offices not actually vacant'.[52]

Since he had gained little recognition for his efforts on behalf of the Tory Protectionists, it was fortunate that in this late Georgian and early Victorian period Lord Salisbury had much of interest to occupy him in Hatfield and the county of Hertfordshire. What is more, the work that he accomplished on his home ground also proved to be of significant worth nationally. From his earliest days at Hatfield he had taken an interest in the poor of the Cecil estates and as a young Member of Parliament for Hertford he had sat on the Poor Law Select Committees of 1818 and 1819. The immediate post-war unrest and the rise in pauperism had bought the issue of poor law reform to the attention of Parliament, and the first Committee was charged with reporting on the defects of the existing system. Its conclusion that the methods of poor relief assessment were actively undermining the profitability and viability of the properties from which the poor rates were raised was received with alarm. One outcome was the Select Vestries Acts of 1818 and 1819, which weighted the voting for vestry appointments in favour of the major landowners and introduced salaried assistant overseers. The system, at first voluntary, grew in popularity so that by the time the Poor Law of 1834 was introduced it had been adopted by more than 20 per cent of parishes in England and Wales.[54] In 1820, while still Lord Cranborne, he contracted with Hatfield parish to run the administration of poor relief for a year.

These early experiences, and his consequent understanding of the issues surrounding the administration of the Poor Laws, undoubtedly underpinned Salisbury's ideas and practice, but he was also influenced by the older paternalist ideals and accepted duties of his class. Lady Gwendolen wrote that 'he lived among his people ... the honour and prosperity of his county, his tenantry, his parish, were as dear to him as his own, – their interests as important to him as they could be to the smallest landowner, to the poorest farmer or labourer in the neighbourhood.'[55] The plaudits of a loyal granddaughter, maybe, but Salisbury's actions, contributions to debates and letters bear witness to a genuine concern for the poor, in particular for the lot of the agricultural labourer. Taking part in the Lords debate on *The State of the Nation'* in early 1830, he spoke with passion about 'the severe distress existing in the country'. There were, he claimed, 'hundreds of able-bodied labourers ... compelled to have recourse to a pittance derived from the parish for their existence', and he moved 'for the appointment of a select committee to inquire into the cause of the distress under which the labouring population were suffering'.[56] In a following debate on the *The State of the Labouring Classes'*, he took the Duke of Buckingham to task for suggesting 'that the labouring classes felt less distress than any others; that as long as the Poor-rates existed they had no reason to complain'. What is more, Salisbury had done his homework well before the scheduled debate. He had 'applied to every parish in the county in which he lived in order to obtain the number of persons unemployed. ... and the number of the working classes out of employ in the county amounted to the alarming sum of 2,200 persons, being six and a quarter per cent of the males, or three and a half per cent of the whole population'. This he claimed might be translated into a national unemployment number of 170,000 able bodied men.[57]

In November 1830, a bill on the Employment of Labourers was brought to the Lords by the Earl of Winchilsea. The emphasis of the debate centred on the great abuses in the administration of the Poor-laws, their original intention 'to give relief to all those who were unable to help themselves' and not to 'stout and able-bodied men', and the question of how 'to provide employment for the labouring classes; so that they might be enabled to get an honest subsistence, and not be thrown on the poor-rates for support'. When Winchilsea's summary was followed by a statement by Lord Suffield that insufficient wages were caused by the 'superabundance of labourers above the demand for labour', Salisbury rose to contest sharply 'the opinion that want of employment arose from over-population'. Neither, he said, could he 'agree to any plan for transporting the agricultural labourers, whom, notwithstanding their demoralisation, he considered to be the most valuable part of our population'.[58] He used the occasion to give notice, once more, of his intention to bring a motion for a committee to inquire into the Poor-laws and this he did less than three weeks later.

In his opening speech Salisbury pointed to the evils endured by the agricultural labourer: the extravagant rate of house rent, the loss of sedentary employment for his family, improvements in agriculture, and the falling by the wayside of the old custom of providing employed peasants a cottage to live in, and a garden and a piece of ground to cultivate. He also raised the issues of the law of settlement and the state of the bastardy laws. He concluded 'by moving for a Select

Committee, to take into consideration the present state of the Administration of the Poor-laws, and to report thereon to the House'. The motion was roundly supported by Earl Grey, who urged 'that their Lordships would acquiesce in the motion of the noble Marquis', there being in his opinion no more important subject for the scrutiny of a committee of the House. The motion was agreed to and the Committee appointed. Grey, also made the point that this should not inhibit the Government from pursuing any aspect of the matter in the interval between the appointment of Salisbury's committee and any ensuing report to Parliament.[59]

It was in no small part due to Lord Salisbury's persistence that the Government did just that and took on the issue of Poor-law reform; beginning with the Chancellor of the Exchequer, Lord Althorp, announcing in February 1832 that a Royal Commission was to be set up to carry out a nationwide investigation into the working of the poor-laws. Twenty six assistant commissioners were appointed to carry out in-depth inquiries and to report their findings to the Commission. One of the most prominent of these was Edwin Chadwick, an acolyte of Jeremy Bentham, who was quickly promoted to the rank of Commissioner.

During the two years between the setting up of the Commission, its report to Parliament and the 1st Reading of the 1834 Poor Law Amendment Bill, Chadwick effectively used the 2nd Marquess as an unpaid consultant to the Commission. It was not just because of Salisbury's commitment to the issue in the Lords, but because of his known commitment and experience in the management of the poor of the estates of Hatfield. Once again the archived correspondence is invaluable. In October, 1833, Chadwick wrote to Salisbury acknowledging the work which he had carried out in the Lords and in the Hatfield parishes. He had written to Hertingfordbury, Bayford, Sandridge, Essendon, Little Berkhamstead and Welwyn and in every case they had been reported as having attempted to introduce Salisbury's plans.[60]

The clearest exposé of the strategies he had introduced to mitigate the lot of the poorest within his estates is provided by the correspondence regarding the poor of Little Hadham. The vestry minutes detail the plan whereby every farmer in the parish would employ one able-bodied labourer for every 25 acres and one lad for every 15 acres. The incentive offered was that each participating farmer would be granted a reduction in rates and in due tithes.[61] A further plan introduced in Little Hadham was for one of Salisbury's farms to be divided into small allotments, 'furnishing them with stock and the means of cultivation for the first season'. The parish rector, reported on the success of the scheme. 'Your Lordship's liberality in taking off so many labourers from the Parish to employ them on the Bury Farm has had an admirable effect', he wrote. 'The farmers instantly divided the remaining number amongst themselves … and there is not now I believe one able bodied man upon the roads'.[62]

As with the best laid plans, not everything went forward without complication. But hearing of complaints from some of the labourers that 'by the hardest labour beginning almost before daylight they could earn 1/9 a day, which they said was worse than working in the gravel pit,' Salisbury refused to accept defeat. 'It is not to be expected that a population degraded by a parish allowance received in idleness although half starved upon it will at once return to industrious habits', he said. 'Time must be allowed to them to shake off their indolence and alter their habits and nothing but necessity will make them do so'.[63] The strategy for keeping able-bodied men employed was still functioning at Little Hadham three years later.

A battle which Salisbury fought with some success in Little Hadham and other parishes was against the practice of adjusting wages in favour of married men with children. Salisbury was adamant that single men carrying out the same work as married men with families should receive the same pay, and made his continuance of the scheme for employment contingent on strict adherence to this principle. He was not prepared to 'be a party to any arrangement which has for its object to reduce the wages of labour under the spurious pretence of relieving men with large families.'[64]

Early in the protracted correspondence between Chadwick and Lord Salisbury, the Commissioner was keen to elicit approval for the broad principles underpinning the report which he co-wrote with his colleague Nassau Senior, Professor of Political Economy at Oxford. Two months before the Poor Law Amendment Bill was brought to the Commons, he wrote to Salisbury of the Commission's agreement that proven ways of administering the law for relief and for diminishing parochial rates should be applied in all other parishes and districts according to their circumstances. No doubt trying to ensure Salisbury's support in the Lords, he went on to claim that 'the modes to which we cleave are those of Hatfield ... so that we hope that your Lordship will find that in legislating for Hatfield Workhouse you have been legislating for the whole kingdom'.[65] But Lord Salisbury was not to be bought with flattery and when the Bill failed to meet all of his objectives, his reservations were made perfectly clear.

In the November 1830 debate in the Lords, which had led directly to the setting up of the Commission, its report and the Bill now progressing through Parliament, he had argued that three things should be addressed in order to improve the lot of the agricultural labourer: the method of administering the Poor-laws, the Law of Settlement and the state of the bastardy laws.[66] When the Earl of Malmesbury introduced the new Bill, which he reminded them had remained under discussion in the other House for no less a period that seventy-six days, he said that it embraced all three distinct subjects. On the first, though, the proposals led Salisbury to believe 'that the principle of the Bill was nothing more than to institute a Central Board of Commissioners, and to take the management of the poor out of the hands of their natural guardians, and to give it to these Commissioners. More was proposed to be done than was necessary for the advantage of the poor, and an immense patronage was to be created, which was not required'.[67] To a paternalist like Salisbury, of course, the natural guardian of the poor was the local landowner and local magistrate, and he was not about to see a diminution of his own role. In Committee he argued that the Bill granted 'a vast extent of discretionary power to the Commissioners, while the Magistrates had only a restraining power over the overseers.' He did not object to the overall superintending power of the Commissioners, but he resisted placing all of the power in their hands.[68] He was also deeply opposed to the clause proposing to take away the power of magistrates to order out-door relief.[69] While unsuccessful in seeing off these clauses altogether, Salisbury, and his supporters who championed the powers of the local magistracy, did force a considerable degree of compromise. The proposal to end all outdoor relief from the following summer was dropped altogether,[70] and even though Poor Law Guardians were elected in each Union, local magistrates became *ex officio* Guardians and continued to make decisions on the administration of relief.[71] Salisbury, himself, continued to control relief in the Hatfield Union, despite Chadwick's continuing efforts to get him to conform. In late 1838, he wrote to let Salisbury know that peremptory orders for the discontinuance of outdoor relief to the able bodied had been issued to seven of the Hertfordshire unions, including Welwyn and Barnet. The order had been suspended respecting Hatfield, though, to give Salisbury the opportunity to explain if there were any grounds for exception. These there were, and explained in detail. 'The workhouse will become too popular', Salisbury replied, giving a forceful example to support his argument. 'I yesterday sent to gaol two men whose avowed object was to get into it for the winter under the plea of neglect of work and vagrancy. They had made themselves liable to the charge and I could therefore do so'. If the order had been peremptory, he explained, the men would have had to be admitted to the workhouse permanently. As it was, they could be admitted for just one night and then sent back to the work which they had deserted.[72] Chadwick and the Assistant Poor Law Commissioner, Colonel Wade, charged with dealing with this situation did not give up, but neither did Salisbury, who continued to administer the law as he felt appropriate and to argue strenuously against developments which undermined his freedom to apply relief flexibly and according to individual circumstances. On the other hand, the principle of less eligibility, "that the condition of the pauper or person subsisting on charity should not on the whole be more eligible than the condition of the person subsisting on his own resources or than the self-supporting labourer of the lowest class", which he and Chadwick had agreed should be the governing principle of workhouse administration,[73] was to prove unworkable. The condition of the independent labourer was so poor in the late 1830s and early 40s that less eligible conditions would have been considered inhumane even by the harshest of Guardians.[74]

Salisbury's push for the bastardy laws to be reformed met with limited success. He believed that the laws were defective in that no man in the humbler stations of life could escape imprisonment, as the consequence of not making provision for his offspring, unless he consented to marry the mother regardless of how improvident such a union might be.[75] The Bill went too far in the other direction, though, and placed full responsibility for bastard children upon their mothers. The compromise finally reached in the Lords was moved by Wellington. Affiliation actions were allowed only if brought before quarter sessions, and any awarded maintenance payments were to cease when the child was seven.[76]

The third area of contention, the Law of Settlement, was not properly addressed at all. It was not until 1846 that Parliament gave relief to the parish of birth and security to labourers who had moved to a different parish for work, by making them permanently irremovable if unemployed once they had resided in the new parish for five years.[77]

The passing of the Poor Law Amendment Act did not mark the end of the correspondence between Salisbury and the Commission. An ongoing issue was the size of workhouses. On receiving details of the proposed Hatfield Union, which joined Hatfield with Welwyn, he wrote to Assistant Poor Law Commissioner, Daniel Adey, with the 'earnest entreaty that we may not be condemned to it. It is by no means our desire to be united to any other parish. ... It will give us much trouble for other parishes are hardly in a state to be joined to us, but the addition of about the worst population in the County could throw us back at least twenty years.'[78] Just what the parish of Welwyn made of this is not revealed, but a quick response from Adey soon set Salisbury's mind at rest and showed just how much influence he still wielded in the interpretation of the new law. 'The public and more particularly myself', Adey wrote, 'are too much indebted to your Lordship for the example you set so many years ago, for me to press anything on the Board that is disagreeable to you'.[79] The final compromise of a small union consisting of only four parishes was reportedly still functioning as Lord Salisbury intended at the time of his death more than thirty years later.[80]

In the early days following the passing of the Act he was once more in discussions with Chadwick, this time on the question of mendacity. Again Salisbury was to put his stamp upon the regulations by allowing his ideas for controlling the problem to be trialled in the Hatfield Union. Chadwick, having fleshed out a plan with the Board of Guardians, believed that if it were 'carried out by your Lordship' it would form a precedent for the next important step in poor law administration. The clearance of the mendicants and trampers would be a powerful means for the prevention of crime. He concluded that 'as the Board are desirous that you should take the initiative in the matter I have no doubt of your succeeding as you succeeded when the initiative of the poor law reform in Hatfield was thrown upon you'.[81] As expected, Salisbury ensured the success of the scheme and was able to report back that he had already put the experiment into effect and 'the trampers who pass through the Union have for the most part combined the sale of small articles with the trade of begging and I have no doubt their number is already materially decreasing when they find that their real wants are attended to [by the Union] but that their impositions are no longer profitable.'[82] The third annual report of the Commission stated that wherever the Hatfield mendacity regulations had been followed the example had met with great success.[83]

As a magistrate and, from December 1841, Chairman of the Herts Quarter Sessions, Salisbury took a keen interest in the working of the law and measures for preventing crime. It also gave him wide experience of criminals of all ages and sorts. Clearly, whilst sitting alongside his fellow magistrates, he was constrained to impose the law to the letter and without favour and many of the sentences passed down seem harsh. Particularly in the cases of juveniles he was concerned for their futures after sentencing and in numerous cases he sought to mitigate the hopelessness of their lives. The Tott brothers, one aged sixteen and the other eight, were convicted of felony and sentenced to three years imprisonment. Salisbury successfully put a case to the Home Secretary, Lord John Russell, for commutation. The younger boy was sent to Parkhurst, the reformatory school, on the Isle of Wight for a reduced term of one and a half years. The elder, had his sentence commuted to transportation for seven years. Salisbury was convinced that both boys had acted under the influence of their families and believed that the elder, if sent to prison for a shorter period would soon fall under that bad influence again. Transportation, would 'give the boy the best chance of reformation'. He further 'hoped that he would be placed in as advantageous a situation as the rules of a penal colony will permit and that he might eventually become again a respectable member of society.'[84]

Thomas Braddin, who had stolen wheat from a loft, had his sentence of transportation reduced in response to appeals from his family and from the victim of the crime, known by Salisbury to 'be most highly respectable'[85] But, when Mary Butcher's family appealed for a commutation of her sentence of transportation for prostitution and robbery to a lesser time in prison, Salisbury wrote to the now Home Secretary, Lord Normanby, apprising him of her record and asking him to refuse the appeal. She had been employed by her family who were of bad character, he said, and there was no prospect of her permanent reform if she were to be turned loose on the world in this country.[86] Similarly, when the cases of Emma George and Emma Little were brought before him for felony and were each sentenced to seven years transportation he refused to support an appeal for commutation. Firstly, he said, they had been indicted for four distinct offences, to each of which they pleaded guilty, and they had, moreover, added to the offence 'by endeavouring to corrupt a young girl their fellow servant and to throw the blame on an old man servant of the family'. He could, he said 'anticipate nothing from their restoration to their family but a continuance of crime', and he could not 'therefore recommend these prisoners for any remission of their sentence which should prevent their transportation'[87]

It would seem that Salisbury judged each appeal on its merits, a major consideration in his decision being the kind of family influence an offender would be released to on termination of the sentence. Where, he was convinced that a felon was a danger to society, he showed no mercy. Appealed to in the case of a murderer, named Frost, he replied that while he believed capital punishments in general to fail in their effect, 'if they are ever to be carried into execution Frost's is a case in which no lenity can be shown without great injury to another'.[88]

Further aspects of Lord Salisbury's interest in the poor and in those brought before the bench, were the issues of prison reform and penal servitude, but it was not until his later years in Parliament that he was able to bring his influence to bear upon national policy.

Arthur Wellesley, 1st Duke of Wellington:
after Sir Thomas Lawrence, 1820
© National Portrait Gallery, London

Sir Robert Peel by John Linnell
© National Portrait Gallery, London
Published by Thomas Boys, 1838

Edward Stanley, 14th Earl of Derby,
© National Portrait Gallery, London
by William Walker & Sons, 1864

Edwin Chadwick
© Wellcome Library, London

Lord Salisbury in later years.
With the permission of the 7ᵗʰ Marquess of Salisbury from the
collection at Hatfield House

The middle years of the century began for the Marquess with great sadness and national mourning for his old friend the Duke of Wellington; at the same time, though, he enjoyed great satisfaction in being offered "employment" at last. In February 1852, after more than a decade, the office of prime minister resided in the Upper House and Salisbury took the post of Lord Privy Seal in the Earl of Derby's first cabinet.

The satisfaction this appointment must have brought him was short lived. Disraeli's budget in December of the same year provoked Whigs, Liberals, Peelites, radicals and the Irish Independent Party to unite in opposition, defeating the Conservatives by 305 to 286 votes. Derby had no alternative but to tender his resignation to the Queen[89]. There followed over five years of tenuous political coalition. Two years of Whig/Peelite government took the country into a hopelessly mismanaged war in the Crimea which forced Aberdeen to resign in January 1855. His successor, Palmerston, leading a fragmented Whig Government, concluded the war but was defeated in the Commons in February 1858, following cross-party opposition to the India Bill, outrage at the appointment of Clanricarde as Lord Privy Seal and the introduction of the Conspiracy to Murder Bill in the wake of the Orsini affair.[90] Thus, Derby once more had audience with the Queen and for the second time assumed office as Prime Minister, for the second time with a minority in the Commons.

Also for the second time, Lord Salisbury was offered employment, this time as Lord President of the Council, a cabinet post one rung in the ladder above his previous position as Lord Privy Seal. But this second administration of Lord Derby was to last just sixteen months; falling after an agreed dissolution and a failed plea for unity in the House of

Lords in April left him facing an election with sparse support, and on the recall of Parliament defeat in a vote of confidence.

Following the fall of the first administration, John Croker, Editor of the Quarterly Review, asked scathingly, 'Why did you not die in the Protestant cause – or something that some party could take an interest in?'[91] Harsh words, with some truth in them. Yet, by the time of his second surrender of the premiership, Derby had managed to restore the Conservative majority in the House of Lords, achieved greater unity and discipline in the House of Commons and the party as a whole was united in pursuit of a single aim: moderate Conservative government ensuring 'sound national commerce and the prosperity of the working classes'; overall the 'orderly comfort of the country'.[92]

Salisbury was by this time entering the last decade of his life, a life which was still dedicated to public service. During, between and after his brief periods in office, he was a notable presence in the Lords, contributing to debate on diverse issues of importance: the on-going reform of Parliament and local government; the state of the Thames and its impact upon the health of the capital; vaccination; highways; the metric system; education; foreign policy and the militia.[93]

His own unfailing contribution in the Upper House in support of 'the orderly comfort of the country' was dominated, unsurprisingly, by the continuation of his work to improve criminal justice for the poor. Peel had brought uniformity to the prison system and reduced the complexity of the legal framework with its consequent delays, but he had made no inroad into the question of enforcement. His 'practical mind found it easier to deal with questions of statute and administration than with the principles of punishment'.[94] It was with this failure in particular that Salisbury was concerned and he pursued with dogged determination the issues of transportation, tickets-of-leave, and penal reform.

The problems surrounding the practices of transportation and tickets-of-leave were summarised succinctly by Lord St Leonards who opened the debate in August 1854 with the statement that 'the question "what are we to do with our convicts?" was one of the most important social questions of the day', and then proceeded to show in detail the difficulties presented by the ending of the current system of sentencing convicted prisoners to transportation. The advantages of the system were many: the convicted person's ties with previous associations were broken; control of the convict passed to the colonial government; employment, wages and liberal rations were ensured and the convict had the prospect of bettering his position if he worked hard and honestly. But now the colonists were refusing to accept more convicts and the Government was forced to substitute transportation with penal servitude at home and a ticket-of-leave system which permitted a convict to work anywhere in the country under such conditions as the Government thought fit. This was all very good in theory. In practice, there was now no inducement for a convict to lead an honest life and, at a time when the demand for labour was less, work was almost unattainable if a person was known to have a ticket-of-leave. St Leonards also complained that no check was kept on the numbers who had been released under the ticket-of-leave system and then committed further offences. He calculated that some 150 convicts a month were "let loose on society" with no provision for control.[95]

As Chairman of Quarter Sessions, Lord Salisbury had shown himself to be a firm supporter of transportation in that it removed the offender from bad influences, and this was reflected in his sentencing of those brought before him. He reminded their Lordships that 'the persons generally sentenced to transportation were not prisoners brought up for their first offence, but mostly belonged to a class of criminals who were thoroughly initiated into a course of vice and crime'. Because of this, he stressed, 'the reform of the offender was a consideration that ought not to be overlooked, and one quite as important as was his punishment'. He advocated that the ticket of leave system should be given a fair trial and then be reviewed by Parliament.[96] Eighteeen months later, this issue of review was taken up by Viscount Dungannon who moved an address for returns on Orders of Licence granted, numbers convicted of subsequent offences, numbers of Licences revoked and numbers of convicts whose licences had been refused or revoked in consequence of their misconduct. In the event it transpired that such returns had already been ordered to be laid before the Commons and it was accepted that these would be sufficient for the purpose of the Lords. A further question put forward was whether production of the returns would be taken up by their Lordships by way of a Resolution bearing upon the subject? Earl Granville's answer that this could only be effected by an Act of Parliament was quickly rebutted by Salisbury who said that 'it was in the power of Government to diminish the evil, by placing these persons under the surveillance of the police, and no Act of Parliament was required to enable them to do that'. He was in no doubt that the Government should do just that since 'as chairman of quarter sessions, he could bear personal testimony to the evil consequences of the system at present pursued'.[97] A few weeks later he again took issue with Granville.[98] It seemed to him, he said, that the assertion that an Act of Parliament would be needed to change the present system, 'had been rashly made, and that the noble Earl, anxious to get rid of a disagreeable subject, answered too hastily ... the noble Earl could not have attentively considered the question, or he would have seen that the present system of granting licences to convicted persons was not that which was recommended by Parliament in the Act passed for the purpose.' He referred back to the Act of 1853, which intended that there should be three grades of probation for convicts: those sentenced to close imprisonment and hard labour for an indefinite period, those sentenced for a certain period and those given tickets-of-leave. For the last category a further clause provided that where a ticketed person could not find honest employment, employment should be found on public works. These provisions, he said, had not been effected. He concluded by clarifying that his object 'was to ascertain upon what principle, and under what circumstances, the ticket-of-leave system was administered, and licences granted to persons who had been convicted of crime'. He wanted to know 'what became of the clause in the Act of Parliament to which he had referred, and why its operation had been so effectually suspended?' While Salisbury had clearly done his homework where the Act itself was concerned, he had been somewhat lax in his selection of a sample of returns put together to press home his point; for, as the Duke of Argyll was quick to point out, only three of the cases had any reference to the Act, and claimed that rather than support the Marquess's demand for returns they showed that the system was, on the whole, working satisfactorily. Despite this, Salisbury's case, was supported by Earl Stanhope and, although the motion for returns was withdrawn, the issues of tickets of leave and of secondary punishments to replace transportation had been fully aired and continued to be a major issue for debate in both Houses.[99.] Indeed, when, three weeks later, nothing had been done to appoint a Select Committee, as had been moved by Stanhope, Viscount Dungannon confronted the House with the truth that 'unless some decided steps were speedily adopted, the Session would pass away without anything being done … [and] it was absolutely essential for the public good that some change should be made. He moved 'That experience has proved the present system of granting Tickets-of-Leave to convicts to be injurious to the interests of society, dangerous to the security of property, and tending to the increase rather than the diminution of crime; it is therefore most important and desirable that Her Majesty's Government should take the matter into their serious consideration, and devise some means, either by providing employment for convicts so released at home or in the colonies, or otherwise, of relieving the public and the country from a most fearful and growing evil.'[100] Dungannon indicated that he would not press the motion if he was assured that no delay would take place in the appointment of a Committee of Enquiry. Salisbury was quick to support his 'noble friend' with the assertion that if he did forbear to press his motion nothing would be done with reference to this subject during the present Session. Having received assurances Dungannon withdrew the motion and on 23 May a further motion to the same effect was agreed and a Committee drawn.[101]

Nine months later in February 1857, Lord Salisbury, undaunted by his previous humiliation, again rose to move the appointment of a Select Committee; this time to consider the question of secondary punishments. Again he was thwarted, but again he pushed the House into a meaningful debate upon the issues and was clearly much delighted to remind the House that the Home Secretary, Sir George Grey, had been compelled to alter his opinion that the ticket-of-leave system was 'perfectly successful' and the objections to it 'an imaginary grievance'; so much as to introduce a Bill on the subject. Judging from the tenor of the Secretary of State's speech Salisbury was sure it was likely to need much amendment, but a further proposal for reformatory schools and the opening of debate on the issue of prison discipline won his full approval.[102]

Finally, in June 1857, The Transportation and Penal Servitude Bill reached Committee in the Lords, where Lord Salisbury summarised the frustration of many of his fellow peers at the apparent disregard of the concerns which had been voiced many times. He reminded the House that 'the insecurity of life and property after the establishment of the ticket-of-leave system was so great, that Committees of both Houses of Parliament were appointed to investigate the matter, and they agreed in the necessity of the reinstatement of transportation'. With unconcealed sarcasm, he then went on to say that 'the Bill carried out that recommendation in rather a singular way, as it commenced by enacting that thenceforward no person should be transported'. It had, he said 'entirely lost sight of the object for which the subject had been brought under the consideration of Parliament, as it did not contain a word about the ticket-of-leave system.[103]

One week later the Bill passed its Third Reading and the Penal Servitude Act came into being, whereby sentences of transportation were abolished and sentences of penal servitude substituted. Provision was made for magistrates to recommit convicts whose licences had been revoked to penal servitude in any convict prison.[104]

It followed inevitably that the issue was not closed, the increase in convicts serving sentences in gaols and houses of correction bringing attendant problems. Returns introduced into the debate on prison discipline in February 1863, showed that there were 148 gaols in England to which 13,000 prisoners had been committed during the previous year. This figure together with the numbers of summary convictions gave an average daily number of prisoners as 16,000 to 17,000. These returns, which related to the year 1860-1 'showed a startling increase in crime' in almost every head of criminal offence'. The issues requiring attention were: lack of discipline; the interpretation of sentences of hard labour; the differing diets; the use of corporal punishment; solitary confinement; and overall, the purpose of imprisonment. A select committee was appointed to consider and report on The Present State of Discipline in Gaols and Houses of Correction, to which Lord Salisbury was appointed.[105] One year later, he was prominent in pushing for returns and for information on whether and what steps had been taken to carry out the recommendations of the Commission on Penal Servitude.[106] It must have been to his satisfaction that in June 1864, following the Report of the Commissioners, the Penal Servitude Acts Amendment Bill reached a realistic compromise regarding both tickets-of-leave and transportation, by legalising and encouraging what had become practice, the voluntary emigration rather than transportation of convicts released on licence.[107]

In 1864 the 2nd Marquess was nearing his seventy third birthday and was very much the old man of the House. His was a constant presence, always demanding returns to inform debate; but by the time the issues of prison discipline were being aired his frailty was beginning to show. The minutes of the debate of February of that year record that 'the noble Marquess, in moving for the Returns, addressed their Lordships at some length, but his observations were inaudible'.[108] Frailty notwithstanding, Salisbury continued to the very end of his life to fulfil his duty as a peer of the realm. Between this first observation of his failing health and his death in April 1868, he was reported as in Division or Committee debating the full range of government business: Foreign Policy, Local Government Reform, Parliamentary Reform, Duties and Rates, Tithe Commutation and issues and emergencies in domestic affairs. He sat on Select Committees covering the Elective Franchise in Counties and Boroughs, the Tithe Commutation Bill, Offices of Parliament, the Cattle Plague Bill and, lastly and most fittingly, on April 02 he was referred to the Select Committee for Poor Relief. On April 03 he was present for the last sitting of the House of Lords until April 20th. He died on Sunday, April 11th.[109]

"The Marquess of Salisbury is dead", wrote the Times the following day.[110] In Hertfordshire, 'where the noble Lord occupied so commanding a position and exercised so vast influence, and where he had only a few days before been seen exercising his public functions with his accustomed energy' the announcement 'excited not merely regret but surprise', wrote the Hertford Mercury. 'Only on Monday week he was amongst us, presiding over the parliament of the county, and still later – but the Thursday before ... he sat for four hours at the meeting of the River Lea Trust conducting its proceedings with his usual ability, and with an energy which seemed to be incapable of growing weary.[111] Then, the Standard's tribute, which Lord Salisbury would surely have appreciated most of all; 'The late Marquess was in every way an important man to his party ... he played a very considerable part in public affairs ... he bore his high office uprightly, and discharged his obligations with zeal, courage and fidelity ... to the last he was a fervent and consistent supporter of the Conservative cause.[112]

He was indeed a true English nobleman.

Author's Note

The correspondence from which this study has been drawn has been focused largely upon the more personal aspects of Lord Salisbury's life: his family, with the responsibilities, disappointments and frustrations of a husband, a father, a brother and a cousin; his love of the family home at Hatfield and his determination to preserve it at all costs; his paternalistic fulfilment of the duties which he associated with his heritage and his class, and which underpinned his political pursuit of legislation for the needs of the poor of the 19th century English rural and urban communities.

I have made a number of references to the archive at Hatfield from which his character in these respects emerges. This archive, which has been preserved at Hatfield House by the generations of the Cecil family for more than four hundred years, is of great importance nationally and an invaluable resource for historians. I am, therefore, extremely grateful to Robin Harcourt Williams, Archivist and Librarian at Hatfield for many years, not only for assisting me in accessing the archive and for reading and commenting upon drafts, but also for agreeing to write the Epilogue to my book. This places the 2nd Marquess within a much wider archival context and throws light upon some further aspects of his life and work. The Epilogue is referenced at the end of the main references section.

Epilogue

The outstanding importance of the archives preserved at Hatfield House is well recognised. Like many other historic estates, Hatfield has accumulated long runs of manorial court rolls, accounts, rentals and deeds relating to properties scattered throughout the kingdom, from St. Michael's Mount in the south-west to the island of Rum in the Inner Hebrides. What makes this archive exceptional, however, is the presence of the very extensive official and personal correspondence of several remarkable members of the Cecil family who held the highest offices of state: they were William Cecil, Lord Burghley (1520 – 1598), Robert Cecil, First Earl of Salisbury (1563 – 1612) and Robert Gascoyne-Cecil, Third Marquess of Salisbury (1830 – 1903).

Other Cecils besides them have achieved distinction in politics. The Hatfield archives contain the personal papers of no fewer than six descendants of the First Marquess of Salisbury (1748 – 1823) who have served in Conservative cabinets in the last two centuries. The Cecil Papers, as the official and political papers of the Elizabethan and early Stuart period are known, have long been consulted by historians. Transcripts of selected documents covering the years 1542 – 1570 were published in 1740 by Dr. Samuel Haynes, tutor to the Sixth Earl of Salisbury. The collection was catalogued between 1829 and 1831, and was afterwards comprehensively described by the Historical Manuscripts Commission in their *Calendar of the Salisbury (Cecil) manuscripts,* which was published in 24 volumes between 1883 and 1976. Besides the official papers, an important collection of early manuscript maps and architectural drawings which belonged to Lord Burghley and Sir Robert Cecil is preserved at Hatfield. There is also a library of their printed books, numbering about 1200 volumes, which has remained largely intact since it was first listed in 1615, soon after the death of Sir Robert Cecil.

Amongst such riches the papers of the Second Marquess (hereafter referred to as "Salisbury") are not pre-eminent. They reflect his comparative lack of success in politics: it is striking that the volume of his correspondence increases markedly only during the periods when he held cabinet office, which was in the short-lived administrations of Lord Derby in 1852 and 1858 – 59. Nevertheless his papers are useful and extensive. The majority are arranged in a chronological "General" series and are not classified by subject. Separate classes of correspondence exist for Salisbury's principal properties and estates: apart from Hatfield these were situated in central London, Cranborne in Dorset, Ilford and Hornchurch in Essex, Liverpool and the Scottish island of Rum.

Naturally the General series of correspondence covers subjects too varied to enumerate. There is a consistency, however, in Salisbury's approach to matters of special concern to him, about which he held strong views. Fortunately it was his habit, when answering a letter, to endorse it with a copy of his reply. Above all he believed in the maintenance of the existing order and in support for institutions such as the army and the church. Many of his answers to letters reveal his ideas about the established hierarchy, which he saw as under threat. A good example is the reply which he wrote in 1852, when he was a minister in the cabinet, to Lord Verulam about appointments in the revived Hertfordshire Militia: "My only feeling is to have an aristocratic County Regiment … Every day increases my conviction that the government of the country is rapidly falling out of the hands of the country aristocracy. Centralisation is become to a certain degree necessary, but a central power is vested in the government of the day and the question is whether the government is to be a King or a Democracy".[1]

Salisbury was a lifelong and generous supporter of the Tory party. In the turbulent period leading up to the 1832 Reform Act he attempted to dominate the representation of the borough of Hertford, which returned two members to parliament, partly by adding to his property in the town. This is reflected in his correspondence, particularly with his solicitor and political agent, George Nicholson. He also took the lead in choosing Tory members to sit for the county of Hertfordshire, as attested especially by his correspondence with three of them, the Hon. Granville Ryder, Sir Henry Meux and Sir Edward Bulwer Lytton. By the time of the 1857 election it was apparent that Sir Henry Meux was becoming insane but no alternative candidate was found and Sir Henry was re-elected and continued to serve for another two years!

Salisbury regarded the Duke of Wellington as his political leader but had a strained relationship with Sir Robert Peel, from whom he failed to receive the employment for which he hoped. In 1841, as some compensation, Peel gave him the Lord Lieutenancy of Middlesex. As Lord Lieutenant he appointed both magistrates and Deputy Lieutenants of the county, a process which generated considerable correspondence. The Lord Lieutenant was also responsible for the control of local military forces, a duty which Salisbury undertook with vigour. He was in his element at the time of the Chartist emergency in 1848. Much correspondence relates to the appointment of special constables to protect London. Ammunition was withdrawn by the militia from the Tower of London for the defence of the British Museum and in April the Secretary of the Trustees wrote to thank him for his frequent visits to the museum and for the care which he had shown for its preservation "on the occasion of the threatened disturbance".[2] Shortly afterwards the Director, Sir Henry Ellis, thanked him for providing protection on Whit Monday, a day when it was not unusual to expect 30,000 visitors.[3]

Throughout his life Salisbury was firmly attached to the established church. He was in regular correspondence with the incumbents of the many parishes of which he was patron or where he owned property. Seldom would an appeal for financial help towards the restoration of the church building, towards the poor of the parish or toward the building of a school, be refused. He would, however, very often make a criticism of the proposed work, either because of its extravagance or where pew rents were to be charged. As he wrote to the Rev. G. Renaud in 1854: "I have strong opinions upon the point of appropriation of seats. I believe that much of the dissent which exists has its origin in the manner in which the poor are edged out of their rights by their richer neighbours".[4] Whenever contributing towards the restoration of a church, he always insisted that a proportion of the seats should be free. He also argued consistently for the provision of more frequent services in existing churches, "a much cheaper expedient for providing church accommodation than building new churches".[5] Putting this belief into action, he paid for the employment of additional curates in St. Helens, Lancashire, and in Holborn, London.

The efficient administration of the poor law was another of his great concerns. As shown in the section covering Salisbury and the poor, his methods were admired by Edwin Chadwick, a regular correspondent, who called him "the chief parish officer in the realm or at all events one of the most practical whom I have met with".[6] "Practical" was a complimentary epithet sometimes applied to Salisbury and it was deserved. He found himself in demand to act as a trustee to help manage the financial affairs of improvident relatives, such as Lord Ingestre, and he was an efficient Chairman of the River Lea Navigation and of the Regents Canal Company, as also of Hertfordshire Quarter Sessions. Most of his own investments were successful, although as James Lea observed in 1864, during the American Civil War, "I observe you are still gambling in Confederate Bonds".[7]

As the correspondence reveals, Salisbury was practical, too, in his approach to architecture. He took a special interest in the building of decent but economical cottages on his estates. Some of his distinctive cost-saving cottages, with bricks laid on their vertical sides in "rat-trap" bond, still survive in Hatfield. In the 1860s he was an early user of concrete and experimented with building cottages, park walls and even a farmhouse, in this material.

One section of his correspondence relates to Hatfield, where he devoted much energy to improving the House and Park. Little in the House was left untouched, as he set out to recapture its baronial and Jacobean character. In keeping with the spirit of the time, *tableaux vivants* were staged in the Marble Hall in 1833, for which Lady Salisbury and her friends dressed up as characters from the novels of Sir Walter Scott. The gardens, too were restored as Salisbury supposed they would have looked at the beginning of the 17th century. Additional impetus to the restoration of Hatfield House was given in 1835, when the west wing was badly damaged by fire and his mother lost her life in the flames. He acted as his own architect for much of the rebuilding.

The library at Hatfield received its share of his energetic attention. He employed the London bookseller, Charles James Stewart, to catalogue the entire library, comprising both printed and manuscript material. As was the practice in other great archive collections, like the British Museum and the State Paper Office, the papers of Lord Burghley and Sir Robert Cecil were mounted on guards and placed in order in calf-bound volumes. This monumental task was carried out in a remarkably short time, between 1829 and 1831. Stewart continued to be responsible for the care of the library until Salisbury's death in 1868, during which period further manuscripts came to light and were bound like the rest.

By his marriage to Frances Mary Gascoyne, Salisbury became lord of the Liverpool manors of Childwall, West Derby, Everton, Wavertree and Much and Little Woolton. Rapid urban development took place there during his period of ownership and the revenue from rents was increased enormously. The process of development is charted in detail in regular letters from the managers of the estate, John Shaw Leigh, a solicitor previously employed by Bamber Gascoyne, and James Lea, who took over the management in about

1849. J. S. Leigh wrote in 1844 "I am happy to say that the fervor of building still continues and I hope soon to see a large portion of your Lordship's land covered in buildings".[8]

Salisbury was a shareholder in the pioneering and very successful Liverpool and Manchester Railway, which crossed his property. He was present in the Duke of Wellington's party at the opening of the railway in 1830, when William Huskisson, who stepped on to the line to talk to the Duke, was run down by the *Rocket* and fatally injured. In due course, many more railway lines were promoted in the Liverpool area, as well as others crossing Salisbury's property in Ilford and elsewhere, and with experience he became a determined, not to say obstinate, negotiator. When the line from London to York was planned in the 1840s, he managed to ensure that the Great North Road was diverted out of Hatfield Park; although disputes over the building of the new road gave him much stress, in the long term the Park was greatly improved.

Rural poverty in Dorset and ways of alleviating it are revealed in correspondence with successive Vicars of Cranborne. In 1830 Salisbury introduced allotments for poor labourers. Although he made an annual gift of firewood for the poor, the Vicar wrote to him in 1832 "the poor people here are sadly off for fuel. Many are obliged to spend their morning in confessedly stealing from the hedges and Lord Shaftesbury's plantations to boil their potatoes".[9] Salisbury also built a church and, in 1855, a school in neighbouring Alderholt. The first schoolmaster's salary was only £30 a year but, when he left in 1856, the Vicar proposed "instead of paying £30 to an untrained master, to offer £25 to a trained mistress (certificated or registered)"[10] on which Salisbury commented "the demands of schoolmasters are now very exorbitant, in many instances far exceeding the stipends of curacy".[11] This is consistent with the view, expressed on another occasion when he objected to a large sum being spent on a schoolmaster's house, "I object to such an expenditure on masters' houses upon principle. I do not think it desirable that a schoolmaster should be placed in a higher scale of society than the clergyman or curate to whom he ought to be subordinate".[12] As a matter of course, Salisbury only supported schools which taught the doctrines of the Church of England.

A very different estate was the Hebridean island of Rum, which Salisbury bought in 1845 principally for fishing and other sport. He regularly spent the months of August and September there. He owned the entire island and, as his correspondence shows, could enjoy treating it as his own little kingdom. He reintroduced red deer and built a dam to improve salmon fishing. The island was used for rearing sheep and their wool was taken to Liverpool on his own paddle steamer, the *Ramsgate Packet*. Sheep which were not sold in Liverpool were conveyed by train, either to be sold in London or to be kept in Hatfield. Salisbury's vessels had an unfortunate history: the *Ramsgate Packet* collided with Liverpool dock in 1848 and his smack, the *Jenny Lind*, was wrecked in the bay of Arisaig in 1860. Fascinating letter-books covering the period 1846 – 1862 contain monthly reports from the factor on Rum and copies of Salisbury's replies.[13]

From the many thousands of letters which he received, and from the copies of the replies which he wrote, Salisbury emerges as autocratic, obstinate, and domineering but also as principled, honourable, capable and fair. His papers demonstrate his firm adherence to his convictions, his vigorous and effective management of his estates and his considerate treatment of his staff and subordinates. In Hertfordshire, "where", as the *Hertford Mercury* reported on his death, "the noble Lord occupied so commanding a position and exercised so vast an influence", he was in effect the Duke of Omnium.[14] Consequently his papers reveal much about local politics and also about the management of a great estate which comprised both rural and urban property. If not of the same significance as some other sections of the Hatfield archives, they nevertheless have an essential place in documenting a prosperous and generally successful period in the 500 year history of the Cecils.

References

A FAMILY MAN

1. Quoted by Lady Gwendolen Cecil, *Robert Marquis of Salisbury*, Vol. 1, p. 3

2. Cecil, D., *The Cecils of Hatfield House*, pp. 198-204

3. Quoted by Oman, C., *The Gascoyne Heiress*, p. 50.

4. Letters of the Duke of Wellington, Hatfield House: Lord Salisbury to the Duke of Wellington, 05 Sept 1841.

5. Diaries of the 2nd Marchioness of Salisbury, Hatfield House: 02 Feb 1835

6. Cecil, D., *The Cecils of Hatfield House*, p. 187

7. Lady Gwendolen Cecil, *Robert Marquis of Salisbury*, Vol. 1, pp. 4-8

8. Cecil ,D., *The Cecils of Hatfield House*, p. 198

9. Lady Gwendolen Cecil, *Robert Marquis of Salisbury*, Vol 1, pp. 7-8

10. Lady Gwendolen Cecil, *Robert Marquis of Salisbury*, Vol. 1, p. 8.

11. Cecil, D., *The Cecils of Hatfield House*, p. 209

12. Lady Gwendolen Cecil, *Robert Marquis of Salisbury*, Vol. 1, p. 7

13. Quoted by Oman, C., *The Gascoyne Heiress*, p. 294

14. Correspondence of the 2nd Marquess of Salisbury, Hatfield House: The Duchess of Gloucester, Princess Mary, to Lord Salisbury, Oct 12 1839. – 2M/I/1/40/26

15. Correspondence of the 2nd Marquess of Salisbury, Hatfield House: various letters and replies 16 – 27 Oct 1839. 2M/I/1/40/25 – 59

16. Cecil, D., *The Cecils of Hatfield House*, p. 213

17. Correspondence of the 2nd Marquess of Salisbury, Hatfield House: Lord Salisbury to Capt. the Hon. G. Hotham re Chairmanship of Herts. Quarter Sessions, Dec 11 1841 – 2M/I/1/48/64

18. Cecil, D., *The Cecils of Hatfield House,* p. 218, and Roberts, A., *Salisbury: Victorian Titan,* pp. 7-9

19. Correspondence of the 2nd Marquess of Salisbury, Hatfield House: Hope, Henry. T to Lord Salisbury, June 6 1842 – 2M/I/1/51/13

20. Correspondence of the 2nd Marquess of Salisbury, Hatfield House: Hope, Lady Mildred to Lord Salisbury, Aug 4 1843 – 2M/I/1/56/4-5

21. Correspondence of the 2nd Marquess of Salisbury, Hatfield House: Hope, Lady Mildred to Lord Salisbury, Jan 2 and Jan 4 1845 – 2M/I/1/62/1&5

22. Correspondence of the 2nd Marquess of Salisbury, Hatfield House: Hope, Lady Mildred to Lord Salisbury, Oct 13, Oct 17 and Oct 18 1846 – 2M/I/1/68/8,17&19

23. Correspondence of the 2nd Marquess of Salisbury, Hatfield House: Hope, Alexander J. B., M. P. to Lord Salisbury, Jan 7 1848 – 2M/I/1/73/3

24. Correspondence of the 2nd Marquess of Salisbury, Hatfield House: Lord Salisbury to Hope, Alexander J. B., M. P., Jan 9 1848 – 2M/I/1/73/4

25. Correspondence of the 2nd Marquess of Salisbury, Hatfield House: Balfour, James M., M.P. to Lord Salisbury, July 15 1843 – 2M/I/1/55/45

26. Correspondence of the 2nd Marquess of Salisbury, Hatfield House: Lord Salisbury to Balfour, James M., M.P., July 15 1843 – 2M/I/1/55/46

27. Correspondence of the 2nd Marquess of Salisbury, Hatfield House: Lord Salisbury to Queen Victoria, July 18 1843 – 2M/I/1/55/49

28. Roberts, A., *Salisbury: Victorian Titan,* p. 7

29. Correspondence of the 2nd Marquess of Salisbury, Hatfield House: Urquhart, Dr. John to Lord Salisbury, February 11 1833 – 2M/I/1/17/19

30. Quoted by Oman, C., *The Gascoyne Heiress,* p. 179

31. Cecil, D., *The Cecils of Hatfield House,* p. 218

32. Correspondence of the 2nd Marquess of Salisbury, Hatfield House: Lyte, Rev. Henry F to Lord Salisbury and draft reply, November 03 1835 – 2M/I/1/26/45-47

33. Correspondence of the 2nd Marquess of Salisbury, Hatfield House: Lyte, Rev. Henry F to Lord Salisbury, May 10 1836 – 2M/I/1/29/26-27

34. Correspondence of the 2nd Marquess of Salisbury, Hatfield House: Lyte, Rev. Henry F to Lord Salisbury, July 30 1836 – 2M/I/1/30/18

35. Correspondence of the 2nd Marquess of Salisbury, Hatfield House: Lyte, Rev. Henry F to Lord Salisbury, Dec 04 1837 – 2M/I/1/34/75

36. Correspondence of the 2nd Marquess of Salisbury, Hatfield House: Lord Salisbury to Lyte, Rev. Henry F, Dec 06 1837 – 2M/I/1/34/76

37. Correspondence of the 2nd Marquess of Salisbury, Hatfield House: Lyte, Rev. Henry F to Lord Salisbury, Jan 13 1838 – 2M/I/1/35/9

38. Correspondence of the 2nd Marquess of Salisbury, Hatfield House: Lyte, Rev. Henry F to Lord Salisbury, Jan 31 1838 – 2M/I/1/35/23

39. Correspondence of the 2nd Marquess of Salisbury, Hatfield House: Lyte, Rev. Henry F to Lord Salisbury, Oct 20 1838 – 2M/I/1/37/19

40. Correspondence of the 2nd Marquess of Salisbury, Hatfield House: Lyte, Rev. Henry F to Lord Salisbury, Jan 18 1839 – 2M/I/1/38/5

41. Correspondence of the 2nd Marquess of Salisbury, Hatfield House: Lyte, Rev. Henry F to Lord Salisbury, July 29 1840 – 2M/I/1/43/64-65

42. Correspondence of the 2nd Marquess of Salisbury, Hatfield House: Cranborne, Viscount to Lord Salisbury, Jan 25 1847 – 2M/I/1/69/27

43. Correspondence of the 2nd Marquess of Salisbury, Hatfield House: Johnson, Edmund C. to Lord Salisbury, Jan 26 1847 – 2M/I/1/69/29

44. Correspondence of the 2nd Marquess of Salisbury, Hatfield House: Lord Salisbury to Cranborne, Viscount, Feb 22 1847 – 2M/I/1/69/28

45. Correspondence of the 2nd Marquess of Salisbury, Hatfield House: Lord Salisbury to Johnson, Edmund C., Feb 22 1847 – 2M/I/1/69/30

46. Correspondence of the 2nd Marquess of Salisbury, Hatfield House: Johnson, Edmund C. to Lord Salisbury, March 09 1847 – 2M/I/1/69/66

47. Cecil, D., *The Cecils of Hatfield House*, p. 218

48. Roberts, A., *Salisbury: Victorian Titan*, p. 9

49. Lady Gwendolen Cecil, *Robert Marquis of Salisbury*, Vol. 1, p. 9

50. Correspondence of the 2nd Marquess of Salisbury, Hatfield House: Lord Salisbury to the Rev. F. J Faithfull, Nov 13 1836 – 2M/I/1/31/38-39

51. Lady Gwendolen Cecil, *Robert Marquis of Salisbury*, Vol. 1, p. 14

52. R. G. Thorne, *The House of Commons: 1790-1820*. Vol. 111, p. 430

53. Roberts, A, *Salisbury: Victorian Titan*, pp. 15 – 21

54. Lady Gwendolen Cecil, *Robert Marquis of Salisbury*, Vol. 1, pp. 49&50

55. Roberts, A., *Salisbury: Victorian Titan*, p. 23

56. Roberts, A., *Salisbury: Victorian Titan*, p. 21

57. Roberts, A., *Salisbury: Victorian Titan*, pp. 28 – 9

58. Roberts, A., *Salisbury: Victorian Titan*, p. 30

59. Roberts, A., *Salisbury: Victorian Titan*, pp. 32-3

60. Roberts, A., *Salisbury: Victorian Titan*, p. 33

61. Lady Gwendolen Cecil, *Robert Marquis of Salisbury*, Vol.1, p 62

62. Lady Gwendolen Cecil, *Robert Marquis of Salisbury*, Vol. 1, pp. 62 & 65

63. Lady Gwendolen Cecil, *Robert Marquis of Salisbury*, Vol. 1, pp. 62 & 65

64. The last Will of the 2nd Marquess of Salisbury, held in the Archive, Hatfield House

65. Roberts, A., *Salisbury: Victorian Titan*, pp. 101 & 102

66. Correspondence of the 2nd Marquess of Salisbury, Hatfield House: Harris, George to Lord Salisbury, Dec 29 1846 – 2M/I/1/68/80

67. Correspondence of the 2nd Marquess of Salisbury, Hatfield House: Lord Salisbury to Harris, George, Jan 1847 – 2M/I/1/68/81

68. Correspondence of the 2nd Marquess of Salisbury, Hatfield House: Harris, George to Lord Salisbury, Mar 11 1849 – 2M/I/1/76/38

69. The last Will of the 2nd Marquess of Salisbury, held in the Archive, Hatfield House

70. All details regarding the marriage, separation, financial agreements, custody arrangements and litigation in the secular and ecclesiastic courts have been drawn from Stone, L., *Broken Lives: Separation and Divorce in England 1660 - 1857*, Chapter 12: *Westmeath v. Westmeath: The wars between the Westmeaths, 1812 – 1857*.

71. Correspondence of the 2nd Marquess of Salisbury, Hatfield House: Lord Salisbury to the Marchioness of Westmeath, Oct 15 1839 – 2M/I/1/40/24

72. Correspondence of the 2nd Marquess of Salisbury, Hatfield House: Marchioness of Westmeath to Lord Salisbury, Oct 20 1839 – 2M/I/1/40/37

73. Correspondence of the 2nd Marquess of Salisbury, Hatfield House: Faithfull, Rev. Frances J, to Lord Salisbury, Oct 26 1839 – 2M/I/1/40/56

74. Correspondence of the 2nd Marquess of Salisbury, Hatfield House: Lord Salisbury to the Marchioness of Westmeath, June 03 1842 – 2M/I/1/51/4

75. Correspondence of the 2nd Marquess of Salisbury, Hatfield House: Marchioness of Westmeath to Lord Salisbury, June 06 1842 – 2M/I/1/51/14-16

76. Correspondence of the 2nd Marquess of Salisbury, Hatfield House: Lord Salisbury to the Marchioness of Westmeath, June 08 1842 – 2M/I/1/51/17

77. Correspondence of the 2nd Marquess of Salisbury, Hatfield House: Marchioness of Westmeath to Lord Salisbury, June 08 1842 – 2M/I/1/50/20

78. Correspondence of the 2nd Marquess of Salisbury, Hatfield House: Lord Salisbury to Lord Talbot, July 18 1846 – 2M/I/1/67/12

79. Correspondence of the 2nd Marquess of Salisbury, Hatfield House: Lady Sarah to Lord Salisbury, July 20 1846 – 2M/I/1/67/14-16

80. Correspondence of the 2nd Marquess of Salisbury, Hatfield House: Lord Salisbury to Viscount Ingestre, July 24 1846 – 2M/I/1/67/18

81. Correspondence of the 2nd Marquess of Salisbury, Hatfield House: Lady Sarah to Lord Salisbury, July 28 1846 – 2M/I/1/67/23

82. Correspondence of the 2nd Marquess of Salisbury, Hatfield House: Viscount Ingestre to Lord Salisbury, July 28 1846 – 2M/I/1/67/24

83. Correspondence of the 2nd Marquess of Salisbury, Hatfield House: Viscount Ingestre to Lord Salisbury, Sept 16 1846 – 2M/I/1/67/46

84. Correspondence of the 2nd Marquess of Salisbury, Hatfield House: Lord Salisbury to Viscount Ingestre, Sept 25 1846 – 2M/I/1/67/47-48

85. Correspondence of the 2nd Marquess of Salisbury, Hatfield House: Lord Salisbury to Viscount Ingestre, Nov 06 1846 – 2M/I/1/68/32-34

86. Correspondence of the 2nd Marquess of Salisbury, Hatfield House: Lady Sarah to Lord Salisbury, Nov 08 1846 – 2M/I/1/68/36

87. Correspondence of the 2nd Marquess of Salisbury, Hatfield House: Lord Salisbury to the Most Rev. Lord J Beresford, Archbishop of Armagh, Feb 11 1847 – 2M/I/1/69/41-42

88. Correspondence of the 2nd Marquess of Salisbury, Hatfield House: The Most Rev. Lord J Beresford, Archbishop of Armagh to Lord Salisbury, Feb 14 1847 – 2M/I/1/69/46-47

89. Correspondence of the 2nd Marquess of Salisbury, Hatfield House: Lady Sarah to Lord Salisbury, Oct 29 1847 – 2M/I/1/72/11

90. Lady Burghclere, *A Great Man's Friendship*, p. 8

91. Lady Burghclere, *A Great Man's Friendship*, pp. 18 & 19

92. Hibbert, C, *Wellington: A Personal History,* gives details of the numerous liaisons of the Duke of Wellington.

93. Quoted by Oman, C., *The Gascoyne Heiress,* p. 145

94. Lady Burghclere, *A Great Man's Friendship* reproduces the letters from Wellington to Lady Salisbury from 1850-1852.

95. Lady Burghclere, *A Great Man's Friendship,* pp. 15 &16

96. Lady Burghclere, *A Great Man's Friendship,* pp. 37 & 38

97. The Bourne Plate, had been bought by Lord Salisbury from Lady Mary's father, Earl De La Warr.

98. The last Will of the 2nd Marquess of Salisbury, held in the Archive, Hatfield House

99. *The Hertford Mercury*, April 12 1868

HATFIELD A FAMILY HOME

1. Correspondence of the 2nd Marquess of Salisbury, Hatfield House: Hope, Lady Mildred to Lord Salisbury, Oct 13 1846 – 2M/I/1/68/8

2. Cecil, D., *The Cecils of Hatfield House,* p. 197

3. Cecil, D., *The Cecils of Hatfield House,* p.14

4. Cecil, D., *The Cecils of Hatfield House,* pp. 197 & 215

5. Snell, S., with an Introduction by the Dowager Marchioness of Salisbury, *The Gardens at Hatfield,* pp. 20 & 40

6. *The Hertford Mercury,* April 12 1868

7. Correspondence of the 2nd Marquess of Salisbury, Hatfield House: Franks W to Lord Salisbury and reply, Nov 27 1844 – 2M/I/1/61/46-47

8. Correspondence of the 2nd Marquess of Salisbury, Hatfield House: Dimsdale, Baron to Lord Salisbury, Nov 14 1844, and reply, Nov 19 1844 – 2M/I/1/61/39-40

9. Correspondence of the 2nd Marquess of Salisbury, Hatfield House: Lord Salisbury to Giles, F, and reply, Jan 09 1845, and Franks, W., to Lord Salisbury, 28 Jan 1845 – 2M/I/1/62/11-12 & 2M/I/1/62/28

10. Correspondence of the 2nd Marquess of Salisbury, Hatfield House: Lawrence, J to Lord Salisbury, June 09 1841 – 2M/I/1/46/60

11. Correspondence of the 2nd Marquess of Salisbury, Hatfield House: Lord Salisbury to Lyon. J, May 03 1844 – 2M/I/1/59/24

12. Correspondence of the 2nd Marquess of Salisbury, Hatfield House: Rennie, to Lord Salisbury, May 13 1844 – 2M/I/1/59/32

13. Correspondence of the 2nd Marquess of Salisbury, Hatfield House: Astell, W, to Lord Salisbury, Oct 18 1844 and reply of Oct 19 1844 – 2M/I/1/61/11-13

14. Correspondence of the 2nd Marquess of Salisbury, Hatfield House: Lord Dalhousie, Vice President of the Board of Trade to Lord Salisbury, Dec 12 1844 – 2M/I/1/61/56-60

15. Correspondence of the 2nd Marquess of Salisbury, Hatfield House: Lord Salisbury to Lord Dalhousie, President of the Board of Trade, Feb 13 1846 – 2M/I/1/65/46

16. Correspondence of the 2nd Marquess of Salisbury, Hatfield House: Lord Salisbury to Denison, E.B, Feb 1847 – 2M/I/1/69/59-61

17. Correspondence of the 2nd Marquess of Salisbury, Hatfield House: Lord Salisbury to Capt. the Hon. G. Hotham re Chairmanship of Herts. Quarter Sessions, Dec 11 1841 – 2M/I/1/48/64

18. *The Hertford Mercury*, April 12 1868

19. Lord Lieutenant's Records, London Metropolitan Archives, GB 0074 L, Administrative/Biographical History

20. Correspondence of the 2nd Marquess of Salisbury, Hatfield House: Anson, G. E., to Lord Salisbury, Oct 11 1846 – 2M/I/1/68/4

21. Correspondence of the 2nd Marquess of Salisbury, Hatfield House: Anson, G.E., to Lord Salisbury, Oct 15 1846 – 2M/I/1/68/13

22. Cecil, D., *The Cecils of Hatfield House*, p. 215

A TRUE ENGLISH NOBLEMAN

1. *The Times*, April 18 1868
2. *The Hertford Mercury*, April 12 1868
3. Oman, C., *The Gascoyne Heiress*
4. Lady Burghclere, *A Great Man's Friendship*
5. Lady Gwendolen Cecil, *Robert Marquis of Salisbury*, Vol 1, p. 5
6. *The Standard*, April 12 1868
7. Roberts,D., *Paternalism in early Victorian England*, p. 29
8. Roberts,D., *Paternalism in early Victorian England*, p. 30
9. Roberts,D., *Paternalism in early Victorian England*, p. 33
10. Roberts,D., *Paternalism in early Victorian England*, p. 44

11. Correspondence of the 2nd Marquess of Salisbury, Hatfield House: Lord Salisbury to Gleig, Rev. G. R., Jan 17 1840 – 2M/I/1/42/18

12. Roberts, D., *Paternalism in early Victorian England*, pp. 42 & 276

13. Hurd, D., *Robert Peel*, Chapter 8, *The Catholic Breakthrough*

14. Hurd, D., *Robert Peel*, p. 127, quoted from R. Peel, *Memoirs*, Vol. II, p.116

15. Letters of the Duke of Wellington to the Second Marquess and Marchioness of Salisbury, Salisbury to Wellington, March 05 1829

16. Evans, E. J., *The Forging of the Modern State, 1783-1870*, p. 232

17. Evans, E. J., *The Forging of the Modern State, 1783-1870*, pp. 232 &233

18. Hurd, D., *Robert Peel*, p. 132

19. Evans, E. J., *The Forging of the Modern State, 1783-1870*, pp. 259-261

20. Letters of the Duke of Wellington to the Second Marquess and Marchioness of Salisbury, Salisbury to Wellington and reply, Jan 31 1831

21. Evans, E. J., *The Forging of the Modern State, 1783-1870*, p. 263

22. Letters of the Duke of Wellington to the Second Marquess and Marchioness of Salisbury, Wellington to Lady Salisbury, May 09 1831

23. Letters of the Duke of Wellington to the Second Marquess and Marchioness of Salisbury, Copy of letter from Wellington to Lord Strangford, Jan 12 1832

24. Correspondence of the 2nd Marquess of Salisbury, Hatfield House: various letters to Lord Salisbury on the Address against the Reform Bill, Jan 1832 – 2M/I/1/14/1-81

25. Correspondence of the 2nd Marquess of Salisbury, Hatfield House: Salisbury's report to Wellington on his audience with the King, Jan 1832 – 2M/I/1/14/82-85

26. House of Lords Debate, 09 April 1832, vol 12

27. House of Lords Debate, 22 May 1832, vol 12

28. House of Lords Debate, 01 June 1832, vol 13

29. House of Lords Debate, 04 June 1832, vol 13

30. Evans, E. J., *The Forging of the Modern State, 1783-1870*, p. 308

31. Quoted by Oman, C., *The Gascoyne Heiress,* p. 159

32. Diaries of the 2nd Marchioness of Salisbury, held in the Archive at Hatfield House, 14 Dec 1834

33. Diaries of the 2nd Marchioness of Salisbury, held in the Archive at Hatfield House, 20 Feb 1835

34. Diaries of the 2nd Marchioness of Salisbury, held in the Archive at Hatfield House, 08 April 1835

35. Evans, E. J., *The Forging of the Modern State, 1783-1870*, p. 227

36. Evans, E. J., *The Forging of the Modern State, 1783-1870*, p. 313

37, Correspondence of the 2nd Marquess of Salisbury, Hatfield House: Lord Salisbury to Sir Robert Peel, Feb 03 1842 – 2M/I/1/49/29

38. Letters of the Duke of Wellington to the Second Marquess of Salisbury: Salisbury to Wellington and reply, Feb 12 1843

39. Evans, E. J., *The Forging of the Modern State, 1783-1870*, p. 315

40. Correspondence of the 2nd Marquess of Salisbury, Hatfield House: Lord Salisbury to Ryder, Hon. Granville D., M.P., Dec 19 1845 – 2M/I/1/64/51-52

41. Correspondence of the 2nd Marquess of Salisbury, Hatfield House: Ryder, Hon. Granville D., M.P. to Lord Salisbury, Dec 20 1845 – 2M/I/1/64/55

41. Correspondence of the 2nd Marquess of Salisbury, Hatfield House: Mahon, Viscount, M.P. Sec. of Board of Control, to Lord Salisbury, Feb 02 1846 – 2M/I/1/65/31-32

43. Letters of the Duke of Wellington to the Second Marquess of Salisbury: Salisbury to Wellington, Jan 22 1846

44. Letters of the Duke of Wellington to the Second Marquess of Salisbury: Wellington to Salisbury, Jan 04 1846

45. Letters of the Duke of Wellington to the Second Marquess of Salisbury: Salisbury to Wellington, Jan 28 1846

46. Correspondence of the 2nd Marquess of Salisbury, Hatfield House: Lord Salisbury to Ryder, Hon. Granville D., M.P., May 31 1846 – 2M/I/1/66/34-35

47. Correspondence of the 2nd Marquess of Salisbury, Hatfield House: Lord Salisbury to Ryder, Hon. Granville D., M.P., July 04 1846 – 2M/I/1/67/3-4

48. Cecil, D., *The Cecils of Hatfield House*, p. 215

49. Letters of the Duke of Wellington, Hatfield House: Wellington to the 1st Marchioness of Salisbury, Aug 04 1814

50. Letters of the Duke of Wellington, Hatfield House: Wellington to Lord Cranborne, Aug 23 1814

51. Letters of the Duke of Wellington, Hatfield House: exchange of letters between Salisbury and Wellington, Sept 5 1841. Note: it is not clear whether there were two separate requests to Wellington. He was Ambassador to Paris in 1815, though travelled to Vienna for the Congress of that year.

52. Correspondence of the 2nd Marquess of Salisbury, Hatfield House: Lord Salisbury to Sir Robert Peel and reply, April 19 1844 – 2M/I/1/59/14&16

53. R. G. Thorne, *The House of Commons: 1790-1820*. Vol. 111, p. 430

54. A. Brundage, *The English Poor Laws, 1700-1930*, pp.48-52

55. Lady Gwendolen Cecil, *Robert Marquis of Salisbury*, Vol 1, p. 6

56. House of Lords Debate, 25 Feb 1830, vol 22

57. House of Lords Debate, 18 March 1830, vol 2

58. House of Lords Debate, 11 Nov 1830, vol 1

59. House of Lords Debate, 29 Nov 1830, vol 1

60. Correspondence of the 2nd Marquess of Salisbury, Hatfield House: Chadwick, Edwin, Poor Law Commissioner, to Lord Salisbury, Oct 10 1833 – 2M/I/1/19/13

61. Correspondence of the 2nd Marquess of Salisbury, Hatfield

House: Randolph, Rev. Thomas to Lord Salisbury, Dec 11 1830 – 2M/I/1/10/45-46

62. Correspondence of the 2nd Marquess of Salisbury, Hatfield House: Randolph, Rev. Thomas to Lord Salisbury, Dec 23 1830 – 2M/I/1/10/48

63. Correspondence of the 2nd Marquess of Salisbury, Hatfield House: Gordon, J.A., to Lord Salisbury, Dec 24 1830 – 2M/I/1/10/49-50

64. Correspondence of the 2nd Marquess of Salisbury, Hatfield House: Randolph, Rev. Thomas to Lord Salisbury and reply, May 01 1834 – 2M/I/1/21/42-45

65. Correspondence of the 2nd Marquess of Salisbury, Hatfield House: Chadwick, Edwin, Poor Law Commissioner, to Lord Salisbury, Feb 02 1834 – 2M/I/1/20/10

66. House of Lords Debate, 29 Nov 1830, vol 1

67. House of Lords Debate, 02 July 1834, Series 3 Vol. 24

68. House of Lords Debate, 24 July 1834, Series 3 Vol. 25

69. House of Lords Debate, 28 July 1834, Series 3 Vol. 25

70. A. Brundage, *The English Poor Laws, 1700-1930,* p. 68

71. Evans, E. J., *The Forging of the Modern State, 1783-1870*, p. 280

72. Correspondence of the 2nd Marquess of Salisbury, Hatfield House: Chadwick, Edwin, Poor Law Commissioner, to Lord Salisbury and reply, Nov 16 1838 – 2M/I/1/37/40-41

73. Correspondence of the 2nd Marquess of Salisbury, Hatfield House: Chadwick, Edwin, Poor Law Commissioner, to Lord Salisbury, Nov 04 1833 – 2M/I/1/19/30-31

74. Evans, E. J., *The Forging of the Modern State, 1783-1870*, p. 282

75. House of Lords Debate, 29 Nov 1830, Vol. 1

76. Brundage, A., *The English Poor Laws, 1700-1930,* p. 69

77. Brundage, A., *The English Poor Laws, 1700-1930,* p. 103

78. Correspondence of the 2nd Marquess of Salisbury, Hatfield House: Lord Salisbury to Adey, Daniel G., Assistant Poor Law Commissioner, May 101835 – 2M/I/1/25/37

79. Correspondence of the 2nd Marquess of Salisbury, Hatfield House: Adey, Daniel G., Assistant Poor Law Commissioner, to Lord Salisbury, May 12 1835 – 2M/I/1/25/39

80. *The Hertford Mercury*, April 12 1868

81. Correspondence of the 2nd Marquess of Salisbury, Hatfield House: Chadwick, Edwin, Poor Law Commissioner, to Lord Salisbury, Dec 28 1836 – 2M/I/1/31/98-99

82. Correspondence of the 2nd Marquess of Salisbury, Hatfield House: Lord Salisbury to Chadwick, Edwin, Poor Law Commissioner, [Dec 1836] – 2M/I/1/31/104

83. Correspondence of the 2nd Marquess of Salisbury, Hatfield House: Chadwick, Edwin, Poor Law Commissioner, to Lord Salisbury, Oct 14 1837 – 2M/I/1/34/51

84. Correspondence of the 2nd Marquess of Salisbury, Hatfield House: Lord Salisbury to Lord J. Russell, M.P. Home Sec, Jan 19, Feb 15 and Mar 07 1839 – 2M/I/1/38/6, 24 & 47

85. Correspondence of the 2nd Marquess of Salisbury, Hatfield House: Lord Salisbury to Lord Normamby, Home Sec, Sept 17 1840, Nov 05 1840, and Nov 24 1840 – 2M/I/1/43/96; 2M/I/1/44/34 & 52

86. Correspondence of the 2nd Marquess of Salisbury, Hatfield House: Lord Salisbury to Lord Normamby, Home Sec, Mar 28 1841 – 2M/I/1/45/58

87. Correspondence of the 2nd Marquess of Salisbury, Hatfield House: Phillips M. Under Sec. at Home Office, to Lord Salisbury and reply, July 11 1844 – 2M/I/1/60/33-35

88. Correspondence of the 2nd Marquess of Salisbury, Hatfield House: Gleig, Rev.G.R., to Lord Salisbury and reply, Jan 17 1840 – 2M/I/1/42/17-18

89. Hawkins, A., *The Forgotten Prime Minister: The 14th Earl of Derby; Achievement, 1851-1869,* p. 57

90. Hawkins, A., *The Forgotten Prime Minister: The 14th Earl of Derby; Achievement, 1851-1869,* pp. 152-156

91. Quoted by Hawkins, A., *The Forgotten Prime Minister: The 14th Earl of Derby; Achievement, 1851-1869,* p.59

92. Quoted by Hawkins, A., *The Forgotten Prime Minister: The 14th Earl of Derby; Achievement, 1851-1869,* pp. 228 & 234-235

93. Records of the House of Lords, Hansard,1851-1868

94. Hurd, D., *Robert Peel,* pp.78,79

95. House of Lords Debate, 4 August 1854, Vol. 135

96. House of Lords Debate, 4 August 1854, Vol. 135

97. House of Lords Debate, 26 February 1856, Vol. 140

98. House of Lords Debate, 18 April 1856, Vol. 141

99. House of Lords Debate, 18 April 1856, Vol. 141

100. House of Lords Debate, 09 May 1856, Vol. 142

101. House of Lords Debate, 23 May 1856, Vol. 142

102. House of Lords Debate, 12 February 1857, Vol. 144

103. House of Lords Debate, 12 June 1857, Vol. 145

104. Legislation.gov.uk, Penal servitude Act 1857

105. House of Lords Debate, 19 February 1863, Vol. 169

106. House of Lords Debate, 23 February 1864, Vol. 173

107. House of Lords Debate, 17 June 1864, Vol. 175

108. House of Lords Debate, 23 February 1864, Vol. 173

109. Records of the House of Lords, Hansard, 1864-1868

110. Quoted by *The Hertford Mercury,* April 12 1868

111. *The Hertford Mercury,* April 12 1868

112. *The Standard,* April 12 1868

EPILOGUE

1. Salisbury to Lord Verulam, 28 July 1852 – 2M/I/1/96/64

2. Rev. J. Forshall to Salisbury, April 1848 – 2M/III/9/F/3/8

3. Sir Henry Ellis to Salisbury, after Whitsun 1848 – 2M/III/9/F/3/15 & 16

4. Salisbury to the Rev. G. Renaud, 8 May 1854 – 2M/I/1/112/6

5. Salisbury to the Bishop of Exeter, 29 May 1858 – 2M/I/1/139/28

6. Chadwick to Salisbury, 12 Nov. 1833 – 2M/I/1/19/36

7. J. Lea to Salisbury, 14 Oct. 1864

8. J. S. Leigh to Salisbury, 23 August 1844

9. Rev. F. Pare to Salisbury, 21 Dec. 1832 – 2M/IV/2/2/67

10. Rev. W. Randolph to Salisbury, 12 Aug. 1856 – 2M/IV/2/5/77

11. Salisbury to the Rev. W. Randolph, 24 Aug. 1856 – 2M/IV/2/5/80

12. Salisbury to the Rev. G. Yeats, 4 Dec. 1859 – 2M/I/1/155/32

13. Reports from the factor on Rum and Salisbury's replies – RU/1-6

14. The *Hertford Mercury,* April 1868

Bibliography

PRIMARY SOURCES

Correspondence of the 2nd Marquess of Salisbury, Hatfield House

Letters of the Duke of Wellington to the 2nd Marquess and Marchioness of Salisbury, Hatfield House

Diaries of the 2nd Marchioness of Salisbury, Hatfield House

GOVERNMENT AND LOCAL GOVERNMENT RECORDS

Hansard.millbanksystems.com/

Records of the House of Lords, 1851-1868 – General survey

House of Lords Debates: Hansard. 1830, Vols. 1, 2, 22; 1832, Vols. 12, 13; 1834, Vols. 24, 25; 1854, Vol. 135; 1856, Vols. 140, 141,142; 1857. Vols. 144, 145; 1863;. Vols.169; 1864; Vols. 173, 175

AIM25 Archives in London and the M25 area: Lord Lieutenent's Records: 1779-1965; Lord Lieutenant of Middlesex. Ref GB0074L

NEWSPAPERS

Reports of the death and funeral of the Marquess of Salisbury:

The Hertford Mercury, April 12 1868;

The Times, April 18 1868;

The Standard, April 12 1868

SECONDARY SOURCES

Brundage, A., 2002. *The English Poor Laws, 1700-1930*. Basingstoke: Palgrave.

Burghclere, W.A., 1927. *A Great Man's Friendship: Letters of the Duke of Wellington to Mary, Marchioness of Salisbury 1850-1852*. London: John Murray.

Cecil, D., 1975, *The Cecils of Hatfield House*. London:Sphere Books Ltd.

Cecil, G., 1921. *Robert Marquis of Salisbury*, Vol. 1. London: Hodder and Stoughton Ltd.

Englander, D., *Poverty and Poor Law Reform in 19th Century Britain, 1834-1914*. London: Longman

Evans, E. J., 2001. *The Forging of the Modern State, 1783-1870*. Third Edition. Harlow: Pearson Education.

Hibbert, C., 1998. *Wellington*. London: Harper Collins.

Holmes, G. and Szechi, D., 1993. *The Age of Oligarchy: Pre-industrial Britain 1722-1783*. Harlow: Longman.

Holmes, R., 2007. *Wellington: The Iron Duke*. London: Harper Perennial

Hurd, D., 2007. *Robert Peel*. London: Weidenfeld & Nicholson.

Hawkins, A., *The Forgotten Prime Minister: The 14th Earl of Derby; Achievement, 1851-1869*. Oxford: Oxford University Press.

Kidd, A., 1999. *State, Society and The Poor in Nineteenth-Century England*. Basingstoke: Macmillan Press Ltd.

Oman, C., 1968. *The Gascoyne Heiress*. London: Hodder and Stoughton Ltd.

Roberts, A., 2000. *Salisbury: Victorian Titan*. London: Phoenix.

Roberts, D., 1979. *Paternalism in early Victorian England*. New Jersey: Rutgers University Press.

Snell, S., with an Introduction by the Dowager Marchioness of Salisbury, 2005. *The Gardens at Hatfield*. London: Frances Lincoln Ltd.

Stone, L., 1993. *Broken Lives: Separation and Divorce in England 1660 - 1857*. New York: Oxford University Press

R. G. Thorne, 1986. *The House of Commons: 1790-1820*. Vol. 111. London: Secker & Warburg.

ONLINE SOURCES

Oxford Dictionary of National Biography

Stanley [nee SackvilleWest], Mary Catherine. http://www.oxforddnb.com/view/printable/41303.

RCS Plarr's Lives of the Fellows Online

Johnson, Edmund Charles (1822 – 1895). http://livesonline.rcseng.ac.uk/biogs/E002365b.htm.

Census Records

Households in Fore Street Hatfield 1841-1861. http://www.the genealogist.co.uk/search/master/

Lea Bridge Heritage

History of managing the Lea. Leabridge.org.uk.

Index